D0276480

BATSFORD PSYCHOLOGY SERIES

Psychology of Religion

Psychology
of
Religion

Geoffrey E. W. Scobie

Lecturer in Psychology
University of Glasgow

B. T. BATSFORD LTD
London and Sydney

For my wife

First published 1975
© Geoffrey E. W. Scobie 1975

Printed in Great Britain by
Bristol Typesetting Co. Ltd, Bristol and
bound by William Brendon & Sons Ltd,
Tiptree, Essex
for the publishers B. T. Batsford Ltd,
4 Fitzhardinge Street, London W1
and 23 Cross Street Brookvale NSW 2100
Australia

ISBN 0 7134 2959 3 (hardcover)
ISBN 0 7134 2960 7 (paperback)

Contents

1   Introduction: What is Religion?

Two thousand million people or two-thirds of the world's population are affiliated in one way or another to one of the world religions. Despite the common occurrence of religious behaviour, or perhaps because of it, our understanding of religion and especially the psychological processes underlying the phenomenon is extremely limited. This does not seem to be the result of a failure to investigate the problem, indeed there is a wealth of available information. The main deficiency appears to be in the absence of an adequate theoretical framework which can integrate the accumulating evidence into a comprehensible whole.

It is evident that many people have first-hand experience of religious belief and yet this makes it no easier to define. The peculiar quality or qualities which denote a particular activity or belief religious rather than non-religious or irreligious are difficult to identify. This problem of definition is not unknown in other fields of enquiry. Welford (1971)* points out that most skills are not easily communicated through language, so that it is difficult if not impossible to learn to play golf or drive a car simply by reading a book. For the same reason the two well-known psychological concepts, intelligence and personality, are equally difficult to define. Therefore, because most definitions of religion are found to be inadequate in some way they are best viewed as working definitions with restricted application. (It is possible that all definition must be of this kind and that the search for a definition having some absolute quality is doomed to failure.) The working definitions that are available in this area are usually related to the field and discipline of the author and such definitions lose their relevance and application in areas outside their original sphere of influence. The activity of people like Leuba (1912), who collected 48 definitions of religion, may prove of historical interest but it is unlikely to improve significantly our understanding of religion. The subject of definition

* See Bibliography, pp 170–179 for source details.

will be re-examined in a subsequent chapter dealing with the psychological study of religion where a working definition is produced which is simply intended to facilitate understanding of the arguments presented in the rest of the text.

Whatever the definition of religion a number of basic areas or dimensions seem to be involved, and if we accept Glock's (1965) division there are five areas which should be considered : religious belief, religious practice, religious experience, religious knowledge, and religious effects. An examination of each of these areas will give the reader some idea of the wide range of activities which come under the heading of religion.

RELIGIOUS BELIEF

This is a wide-ranging concept dealing with the content, ideas, dogma, and doctrine of religious faith. It involves some degree of personal commitment to such ideas and underlines the theological distinction between intellectual acceptance and faith. Differences in belief represent the principal distinction between the world religions and the divisions and denominations that exist within them. In addition there are certain beliefs which vary within a given religious organisation. For example, the belief concerning the authority of the Church and its clergy varies within Roman Catholicism from a total subservience to all the pronouncements and dictates of the institution, to an insistence on the freedom of the individual to make his own decisions about certain specific issues.

The concept of immortality is another important area where there are significant variations. Some individuals see a belief in an afterlife as an unnecessary adjunct to the belief system while others within that same organisation see it as fundamental to the group's existence. It is not our intention to review all the possible areas of differences in belief but merely to point out that shades of belief constitute an important area of variation. Many investigators have attempted to measure differences in religious belief in order to determine the quality and extent of religious commitment, but as Welford (1971) points out, some of the conclusions are unjustified being based on answers to questions which are intellectually weak and theologically crude such as, ' Do you believe in God?' The answers from the more sophisticated questionnaires which attempt, for example, to ask about the type of God believed in, seem to indicate a change in the quality of religious belief rather than a dramatic change in religious commitment.

In this area of study it is important to bear in mind not only the contents of beliefs, but the manner in which they are held and the consequent effect on behaviour since items of belief in themselves would have little significance if they did not influence the individual to respond in a particular way. In other words religious beliefs should be referred to as religious attitudes because some behavioural element is usually implied.

RELIGIOUS PRACTICE

Within the world religions there is an extensive variety of religious practices, perhaps the most characteristic being some commitment to an organised form of worship. Investigators have regularly used the frequency of attendance at a place of worship as an indicator of religious activity. Surveys using this criterion provide the principal evidence for the suggested decline in religious activity in Britain during recent years. But, as some surveys have indicated (I.T.A. 1970), it is probably the commitment to institutionalised religion which has decreased, while religious attitudes have tended to retain much of their popular appeal.

Worship includes a number of activities which are considered typically religious, such as prayer, the reading of the 'holy' writings peculiar to the group, and the communal or fellowship meal. These three activities show most clearly the distinction between the religious and the purely ethical systems of belief. Some mention should perhaps be made of the christian practice of confession. The ritualistic confession of 'sin' to a priest, a fellow believer, or to God in prayer, supported by the belief in divine forgiveness, provides for many a significant antidote to guilt arising from misdemeanours in daily life, especially when such practices are genuinely and devoutly followed.

Another important area of religious practice concerns the attempt to extend the influence of the religious group. This involves two basic concepts, namely proselytism and evangelism. Proselytism is simply the attempt by members of a religious institution to persuade outsiders to join their group. It stresses the importance of outward conformity to the group norms and not necessarily a full acceptance of the religious belief system. Evangelism is associated with the Christian faith and involves preaching or proclaiming the good news, the gospel. Evangelism normally emphasises commitment to the Person of Christ as the epitome of the Christian faith rather than commitment to a particular institution or denomination. This probably only involves a change in emphasis and most evangelism usually involves or results in proselytising activities. Under the heading of evangelism within the Christian faith is included the personal attempts of individuals to proclaim their faith, and the large revivalist meetings like Billy Graham's where mass conversion is attempted.

Most religious belief systems include an ethical code and membership of the group involves the practice and observance of the code. The quality of the individual's adherence to the ethical code is often used as a measure of the validity and vitality of religious belief and commitment. Frequently there is some dispute as to the practical application of the ethical code, the more conservative members advocating a rigid and vigorous adherence to the exact letter of the code while the more radically minded members of the group insist on a broader interpretation. This is especially true within Christianity where a radical view of the code of love has produced what has been called the 'New Morality' in contrast to the 'Old Morality', which is seen as a strict observance of the Ten Commandments.

RELIGIOUS EXPERIENCE

A consideration of religious experience takes us into what is perhaps the most important area of religion and, of course, the most difficult to investigate. For many individuals the religious life originates and may be maintained by religious experiences.

One common experience is usually referred to as conversion. It frequently represents the beginning of the religious life. Each conversion experience is undoubtedly unique, but we shall subsequently suggest that they can be assigned to three broad categories : (1) sudden conversion; (2) gradual conversion; and (3) unconscious conversion. The experience is claimed to be of paramount importance in religious belief and behaviour. In consequence it will be examined in detail in a subsequent chapter.

Religious mystical experiences have a profound effect on the lives of the recipients. The vision or voice which the individual perceives often produces a dramatic change in subsequent behaviour. The experience of St Paul on the road to Damascus is a well-known example of this fact. The mystical experience, whether it comes by chance or is sought by stringent self-denial, solitude, fasting, or flagellation, is probably a psychological or physiological phenomenon which is given religious significance by the recipient. The interpretation which the individual gives to the experience is usually responsible for the behavioural changes which may occur. Mystical experiences are relatively uncommon; although many religious people do not appear to have these experiences, even so they remain deeply commited to their faith.

The phenomenon of glossolalia or ecstatic speech is closely related to the mystical experience. Instead of the eyes and ears being subjected to an apparent outside influence, the lips and the tongue seem to be possessed. The experience appears to be quite common amongst Pentecostal churches and sects. There has been very little experimental work done in this area but the four characteristics said by James (1902) to distinguish mysticism seem to apply to glossalalia : ineffability (the subject has difficulty in explaining and describing his experience to others), neotic quality (the individual feels that through the experience he has gained knowledge or understanding), transiency (the experiences are episodic), and passivity (the person feels he is in the grip of a power other than himself).

The number of cases reported of this particular experience and the related phenomena of divine healing has recently increased in such areas as South America and in particular churches in England within the major Protestant denominations. It may well be that the importance of this particular aspect of religious experience will increase in the years that lie ahead.

RELIGIOUS KNOWLEDGE

This is simply an indication of how much a person knows about religion in general or a religion in particular. It is not a question of belief; he may know that Christians believe in the resurrection or the virgin birth, but may not believe it himself. Sometimes it is found that the most committed individuals are not always the most well informed about their religion or denomination.

RELIGIOUS EFFECTS

This final category has already been referred to in connection with the relationship of belief to behaviour, but what was said needs expanding. Glock divides it into two areas which he refers to as rewards and responsibilities. Under rewards he lists those effects with immediate application such as peace of mind, and which are relevant to the future, namely, eternal life, etc. Any reward may have a significant effect on behaviour : many of the accounts of Christian martyrs show the composure that presumably the belief in eternal life and the idea that, ' to be with Christ which is far better ' gives to those facing imminent death. The immediate reduction in anxiety engendered by such a belief can produce quite dramatic behavioural changes as evidenced by the accounts of sudden conversions which are accompanied by the alleviation of a drink or drug problem (Wilkerson 1963).

The acceptance of an ethical or moral injunction by the religious group to which the individual belongs will undoubtedly affect his behaviour. The extent of the behavioural change is an important measure of personal commitment to the religious belief system. The character of the injunction may vary from a concrete situation such as no alcohol to general principles which govern the individual's life situation. In most religious groups there is a mixture of both specific and general types of instruction.

With the exception of the early work by James (1902) Starbuck (1899 and 1926) and Coe (1916), etc. on religious experience, recent work has dealt mainly with religious belief and religious practice, and has tried to relate them to factors of personality. The attempt has met with only limited success and Brown (1962) has indicated that there may not be any relationship beween religious belief and personality at all.

It is the purpose of the present book to examine the research in these areas and to re-emphasise the importance of the religious experience category, especially in connection with conversion and attempts to relate other religious topics to this category.

SUMMARY

In this chapter we have considered the problems of defining religion and concluded that most attempts produce more confusion than clarity. Definition should be seen in a purely pragmatic light, as working definitions relevant within a very restricted area and applicable only to the discipline in operation. In general the scope of religion was organised into five basic areas : belief, practice, experience, knowledge, and effects and a brief indication of the amount of research done in each area was given.

Religion has been studied from many different points of view. Each approach contains its own set of pre-suppositions and biases. Quite often the academic discipline of the author influences the kind of study that he makes, but most investigations come into one or more of the following subject areas : historical, anthropological, philosophical, theological, sociological and psychological. The main emphasis of the present text is on the psychological investigation, with some additional comment on certain of the sociological studies. This chapter will briefly review these varied approaches to the study of religion. It is not the intention to provide a substitute for a more detailed examination of the subject within each of the related disciplines but simply to give the reader a better idea of the contribution that psychological studies make to the total understanding of religion.

THE HISTORICAL APPROACH

Historical studies have in the past consisted of an annotated list of chronological events, what Marvick (1970) has called the 'one darn thing after another' approach. Historians now advocate a more thematic study involving a critical evaluation of the source material and a detailed discussion of possible causal factors contributing to an event or series of events so that any historical document is critically assessed for its validity and reliability in the light of the biases of the author and additional contemporary evidence. Psychological investigations have indicated that in general people are subject to prejudice and predisposition when they study any subject. The modern historian is likely to be under such pressure when he selects material for his analysis. It is possible that given a number of causal variables for an event, like say, the origin of a war or revolution, the personal bias of the author may lead him to single out one variable as more significant than the others. The weighting he gives to this factor may be at variance with other historians in his field. A good example of this is the debate between historians such as A. J. P. Taylor and Trevor Roper over the cause of the Second World War. The main point at issue seems to be the weight that each attaches to the character and aims of Hitler. This one factor, the personality of Hitler, seems to produce a quite different set of conclusions from each of the protagonists.

Historical studies then involve the detailed investigation of source material and the checking of their validity and reliability but some account has to be taken of the personal prejudice of the historians themselves. They must attend to at least three basic aspects of their subject :

(1) Source material – documents, writings of contemporaries, public records, eye witness accounts, etc.
(2) Actual events – civil war, revolution, etc. They have to sift contributory factors and rate their relative importance.
(3) Historians – watch subjective and academic bias in the interpretation of events.

The importance of these aspects can be seen in the historical studies of religion. An example of the first aspect is the source criticism of the synoptic gospels; the second is probably best illustrated by the analysis of the causes of the Crusades; the conflicting accounts of the Reformation from a Protestant and Roman Catholic viewpoint demonstrates the operation of subjective bias in relating and recounting events – the third aspect listed above. All these examples come from the Christian religion but probably similar examples could be taken from the other major world religions.

Investigating the sources of the synoptic gospels is a complex problem which exercises the ingenuity of historian, theologian and archaeologist. It is difficult not only because the events took place nearly 2,000 years ago but because in world terms the place of origin was relatively obscure. This means that references to the events by disinterested chroniclers is rare and the greater part of the evidence is provided by individuals involved in and committed to the ' new ' religion. The historian here is not attempting to build up a picture from contemporary sources but rather to determine the reliability and establish the identity of the witnesses. In other words it is not only the sources but the validity of the authors which is of vital concern. Any assessment of the author of a document demands a clear understanding of the psychological processes which are involved in the perception, memorisation, and recording of events. The problem is analogous to the difficulty that judges and juries now have in assessing evidence provided by witnesses. A full discussion of this modern problem is given by Trankell (1972) in his book *The Reliability of Evidence*. The additional difficulty for investigators of the synoptic gospels is that the character of the original writers is either unknown or incomplete. How closely the record follows the actual words spoken by the original participants remains largely conjecture. These problems have led to the linguistic analysis, textual criticism and demythologising of scholars such as Bultman (1963).

From the above discussion it is apparent that an historical analysis frequently leads to considerations of a linguistic and psychological kind. It is for this reason that history is being more closely linked with the behavioural or social sciences than it has in the past. Certainly the historical studies of religion can be seen as complementary to investigations by psychology and sociology.

The second area of historical studies can best be described as *causal analysis*. A basic assumption seems to emerge, namely that events and their political and military consequences are usually the result of a complex interplay between many factors. This seems to apply even to such dissimilar events as the Crusades and the dissolution of the monasteries by Henry VIII. In each case political and economic factors may have had more significance than the obvious religious variables peculiar to the immediate situation. Causal analysis studies provide a basis for explaining apparent contradictions in the historical picture and for avoiding oversimplification by explaining the situation in terms of only the more obvious factors. The temptation to explain the problems of Northern Ireland as simply a religious conflict between Protestants and Catholics is a case in point.

The third aspect listed is graphically illustrated by the conflicting accounts of successive Protestant and Roman Catholic authors of historical events during the Reformation period. The nature of the written accounts may not be deliberately framed to conceal unpalatable truths, but this is how it often appears to the 'other side'. The author has to select from a large body of information items that he feels are crucial to the circumstances leading to, or arising from, a particular event. These items then form the substance of his book. In a similar way the weight and significance given to an incident will depend on the overall view that the author has of his subject matter. The selection and the weighting of items are to a large extent determined by his biases and predispositions, in this case whether he is a Roman Catholic or a Protestant or sympathetic to one side or the other. Such consideration will determine not only the recording or otherwise of an event but also the amount of detail and emphasis that it receives. Quite often incidents which are detrimental to one side will only be fleetingly referred to in its historical records. With the passage of time and the operation of certain psychological processes these differences become more and more exaggerated until two quite distinct histories or mythologies develop : one peculiarly Catholic and one peculiarly Protestant. The psychological factors principally involved in this process are (1) sharpening, in which certain events or ideas are highlighted and emphasised because they are familiar or significant to that individual; (2) levelling, where unfamiliar events are underplayed and not given the same significance they may have had in the original situation; (3) selective or motivated forgetting, which is the general process of failing to remember unpleasant or dissonant events. It is factors such as these which help explain some of the gross contradictions in the accounts emerging from the two opposing camps.

The social forces, helping to maintain each religious institution, provide the underlying motive power for the three processes mentioned above. It is at this point that the expertise of the historian is invaluable although the task is not an easy one, especially as the status of certain institutions rests on their own particular interpretation of Reformation events. The historian inevitably brings his own set of subjective biases to the situation and these must be allowed for before he can hope to produce an account offering a better understanding of the circumstances and events of the Reformation.

This brief discussion of some aspects of Christianity illustrate the great contribution that modern historical studies can make to a better overall understanding of religion and religions.

THE ANTHROPOLOGICAL APPROACH

In its largest context anthropology is the study of man and therefore includes medicine, human biology, biochemistry, and physiology, sociology, psychology and most of the other social sciences. In practice however anthropolgy has had a more restricted application : traditionally it has investigated primitive tribes. The study has included not only tribes still in existence but those long since extinct and investigated by means of archaeological discoveries. This latter work is one of reconstruction, whereas the former uses the technique of detailed and prolonged observation of primitive societies usually in their own environment. Many tribes have been investigated, but those of New Guinea, North India, and the Australian aborigines seem to have been the most popular. This descriptive study of primitive societies, usually referred to as ethnography, form the principal basis for the anthropologists' claim that his subject is an empirical science analogous, at least in intention, to physics or chemistry. There are a number of separate branches within the discipline :

Physical anthropology is chiefly concerned with the biological and genetic development or evolution of the human species, its ancestry and the development of the human culture. It studies early types of social grouping in human behaviour. It is dependent to a large extent on the work of the archaeologists to provide its basic information. The physical structure and brain size of human or sub-human remains and the inferences that can be made about the kind of life led by such people form its main preoccupation.

Social anthropology in its narrow sense deals with the social structure of primitive societies, but as a wider viewpoint covers all the accoutrements of society.

Cultural anthropology is the study of primitive cultures.

Anthropologists are divided over the definition and application of social and cultural anthropology and quite often they have been used interchangeably. The difficulty seems to lie in producing an acceptable definition of society and culture. Some writers have maintained that it is impossible to separate the two and have preferred the description sociocultural anthropology (Nadell 1951).

It is not surprising that a wealth of information about religious ideas and beliefs arises from anthropological studies of primitive cultures. It would appear that most, if not all, primitive societies have their own religious myths, legends and rituals. These studies have provided much useful information about animism, pantheism, totemism and other varieties of primitive religious belief. It is probably Frazer's book *The Golden Bough* (1929) which gives the classical summary of the work of anthropologists on primitive religion. In general religion is seen as an evolutionary development. Man first worshipped the spirits that dwelt in rocks and trees, i.e. animism. From this he progressed to totemism, where an object or animal became the emblem or symbol of the tribe; and then to pantheism, the recognition of a spirit or being indwelling the whole of nature. There then arose polytheism, the idea that there are many gods, each one with a specific function or location. Monotheism, the concept on one supreme God, represents the height of religious development. A number of alternatives have been proposed to this general scheme, perhaps the most notable of which was a proposal by Marett (1914) who claimed that an earlier stage to animism existed. This stage he called animatism, a belief in the animation of natural objects by the impersonal force of mana. This was quite different from animism which referred to the spirits which activate men, beasts and the objects of nature. The ensuing controversy between the animists and the animatists is now dead, mainly because cultural and religious evolution has been rejected by many anthropologists over the years as an inadequate explanation of the accumulating empirical evidence. There were suggestions put forward of periods of primitive stagnation or retrogression (Leroy 1922) related to what was seen as the degenerating effect of the practice of magic. Instances of primitive monotheism were also cited (Lang 1898) which were inconsistent with the conception of monotheism as the pinnacle of religious evolution. Investigations and theories such as these gradually brought the idea of cultural and religious evolution into disrepute. Also there was the implicit assumption in this theory that religion was gradually being destroyed as man's knowledge increased, but the stress of the emotional and functional aspects of religion again tended to undermine the evolutionists theories.

It is difficult to try and evaluate the present day position on this issue. It would appear that the initial concept was totally inadequate to deal with the multifarious aspects of religion. It is evident that within religious development there are periods of high spiritual insight, periods of stagnation and periods of exploitation when religious leaders use their position for their own ends. Consequently it may not only be difficult but impossible to determine from the available empirical evidence the character of the original prototype religion. It seems an assumption (how be it a reasonable one) to claim that modern religions have evolved from a more primitive variety. Even the idea that early religions were less complex is difficult to substantiate. It is possible that such simplicity is merely an artifact of the selection procedure involved in the data gathering process employed by anthropologists.

The question of the origin and development of religion and its importance and effect on growing cultures seems to be the principal contribution of anthropology to the study of religion.

THE SOCIOLOGICAL APPROACH

Sociology is very closely allied to anthropology. Its principal area of investigation is modern society. It studies the structure and function of modern societies and the numerous institutions and groups which form the constituent parts of each society. It usually collects information by means of surveys which are then subject to statistical analysis. In addition it employs the observation technique of anthropology. It is tempting to state that anthropology studies culture while sociology studies society but in the broadest and most usual sense of these words there is considerable overlap and therefore such a distinction is unhelpful. Even the emphasis on either primitive or modern societies which used to distinguish the two disciplines is losing signficance. The advance of world communication means that the pervading influence of western society has reached many of the existing primitive cultures. They have been significantly altered and no longer provide an uncontaminated source for culture study. Even some of the more remote tribes of the Amazon jungle approach the civilised village communities to barter for steel knives originating from western society. This contrasts quite dramatically with the period of the late nineteenth and early twentieth century when there was little, if any, contact between such tribes and the outside world. In consequence anthropologists have begun to apply their techniques and expertise to modern societies. They have also started to use some of the statistical methods applied by sociology rather than relying entirely on their well tried ethnological system. This means that while there are still some differences in emphasis it is becoming increasingly difficult to differentiate between the two disciplines.

Not only is there no clear-cut boundary between sociology and anthropology but there is a similar problem between the related disciplines of psychology and social psychology. It is usual to consider psychology as the scientific study of behaviour and social psychology as a similar study but applied to the individual in reference to the groups to which he relates. Sociology can then be described as the study of society and the groups which make up society. These distinctions are theoretical, however, for man is a social animal and therefore it is difficult to collect meaningful material about the individual without reference to the social context in which he lives. Similarly it is almost impossible to study groups or society as a whole without reference to the individuals which are its constituent parts. It is therefore possible to find some psychological studies which have a considerable sociological emphasis while some sociological investigations might more easily fall within the realm of psychology. An example of this is the role social class plays in the life of the individual and many of the groups which make up society.

In essence sociology studies the structure and composition of groups. It looks at the pressures and tensions which operate within them and the function and purpose of their existence. It also examines institutions and society as a whole, again, not only determining structure and composition but examining the function that various institutions may have within society. Another major area of study concerns the interaction between one group or institution and another.

It is evident that religion, either as an institution (e.g. the established church) or a group phenomena (e.g. West Indian Pentecostal sects) form an integral and significant part of sociology. For this reason and because of the overlap between sociology and psychology the subject is considered again at greater length in chapter 8.

THE PHILOSOPHICAL APPROACH

The discipline of philosophy studies such topics as metaphysics, epistemology, ethics, aesthetics, and logic. A brief comment on each of these topics will give some idea of the scope of philosophy.

Metaphysics is the subject which deals with problems that lie outside the realm of natural sciences such as physics. It relies not so much on empirical evidence derived from observation and experiment but upon *a priori* grounds of pure reason. Its principal concern is the problem of existence or being. Kant identified the permanent problems of metaphysics as those of God, freedom and immortality. But it could be argued that Kant saw all existence as bound up with the existence of God and this may be an assumption that other philosophers may not wish to make.

Epistemology is the study of knowledge. The problem of how we know and what we know is an intriguing one and embraces aspects of the psychology of awareness. The study seeks to establish the difference, if any, between knowing things and knowing people. Such considerations lead us into the problem of meaning and language. The study of the exact meaning of words and sentences has always been an important part of philosophy and the early logical positivists argued that the sole task of philosophy was an analysis and clarification of language. The logical positivist movement gave way to linguistic analysis which made more modest claims and sought to establish meaning in terms of actual usage rather than on *a priori* grounds.

There is an area of overlap between metaphysics and epistemology in so far that knowledge is sometimes seen as a prerequisite for being and that being and knowing are inextricably linked. This problem has been the subject of much debate from the time of Plato to the present day.

A third area in philosophy is *ethics or moral philosophy*, the systematic study of right conduct. The central problem is to determine what constitutes good, bad, right or wrong. Kant's categorical imperative, the idea of a moral 'ought', which constrains or dictates action is a fundamental concept in the subject. The intention is to create an ethical system which is derived from abstract notions drawn from common experiences. Most traditional theologians would of course maintain this is impossible and insist that ethics can only be derived from the principles of revealed religion.

The subject of *aesthetics* is also related to psychology, in so far as it seeks to determine what constitutes the subjective experience of beauty and to produce theories of beauty; this also forms part of the psychology of perception. The relevance of such considerations to religion and religious experience exist because quite often experiences of extreme beauty lead to religious experiences or are interpreted in a religious way.

Logic forms a substantial part of philosophy. It is the systematic study of the structure of propositions and the observation of general procedures and conditions for valid inferences from them. Logic has developed from a consideration of the syllogism to a more sophisticated system of mathematical or algebraic representation. This is referred to as symbolic or mathematical logic. It uses a propositional calculus which represents an attempt to produce a system similar to mathematical calculus but applied to propositions rather than numbers. In this way the logical operations and the internal consistence of a propositional sequence can be examined. This is essentially a system for deductive logic. There is also inductive logic which forms a significant part of the scientific method. The study of the assumptions, methods and techniques of science is the area considered by the philosophy of science. Its value is that it seeks to remind scientists of the presuppositions and limitations of their science.

Armed with this vast amount of logical argument the philosopher brings his expertise to bear on religion and religious belief. The *philosophy of religion* covers the essence, origin, nature and value of religion and religious experience. There is, however, a division of opinion over the exact nature of the study. Some maintain that the attempts to prove the existence of God and the validity of religious beliefs, apart from revelation, forms the proper subject matter for the philosophy of religion; others insist on the supremacy of revealed truth. In this case the philosophy of religion deals with the basic material of revealed religion and considers the problems it has presented to theology. In terms of the problem of the existence of God this philosophical approach evaluates how man comes to a knowledge of God's existence and what evidence contributes to this apprehension and understanding. The metaphysical problem of God's existence in contrast to other existences is also studied.

Another important activity within the philosophy of religion is comparing the Christian position with other philosophies and religions. Comparative studies of Christian apologists and major philosophers such as Plato and Kant, and the differences between Christian thought and that represented by other religions, forms a substantial part of the philosophical studies of religion.

The principal contribution of philosophy to religion is to examine its logical form, determine internal consistence and determine what other information can be derived from the assumptions and assertions underlying religion and Christianity.

THE THEOLOGICAL APPROACH

Theology is essentially the study of God. It can be divided into two parts : *natural theology* and *revealed theology*. The former develops a body of knowledge about God and His relationship to man and the world by the exercise of human reason only. Natural theology claims to be independent of special revelation and is closely allied to the philosophy of religion as both deal with such things as the existence of God without reference to revealed truth. In many ways it is a subject emanating on the one hand from theology and on the other from philosophy. This fact is recognised by the use of an alternative name, philosophical theology, which emphasises the two roots (Flew and MacIntyre 1955). Opinions are divided about the value of natural theology. For example, it forms an integral part of the theology of Thomas Aquinas and as such has been accepted by Roman Catholics as an important part of their apologetics. In contrast Karl Barth sees little if any use for natural theology, insisting that truth about God is revealed and not derived by reason.

Revealed theology studies the core of truth provided by special revelation. It is generally restricted to the Christian revelation, although theoretically it should be possible to talk about a revealed theology for other religions, especially Islam. Christians assert that Christ is the final and ultimate revelation of God and the truth about God, but this assertion is not accepted by Mohammedans. It would seem in practice however that theology has been restricted to the consideration of Christian doctrine whilst similar studies of other religions have attracted other labels such as 'the principles of religion'.

Revealed theology in this sense has been called the queen of science because it treats its information source (the Bible) in the same way that the natural scientist treats their information source, the natural world. The subject matter is normally divided into six broad areas; the doctrine of God, the doctrine of man, the Person of Christ, the work of Christ, the doctrine of the Church, and the doctrine of the last things. The theologian when studying each of these areas is trying to consider all of the available information both from Old and New Testaments and produce an acceptable explanation (or theory). The theory must be consistent not only with all the information within the area of the study but also with subjects outside of that immediate area. For example, if as a consequence of studying the Person of Christ a theologian insisted that there was no need to postulate the divinity of Christ, he would have to resolve the conflict between this assertion and the work of Christ in redemption and salvation.

THE PSYCHOLOGICAL APPROACH

Psychology as the scientific study of behaviour is concerned with the origin, development and maintenance of an individual's religious belief. It can say nothing about the truth or validity of religion. It may make some assessment of the value of religious belief for the function and stability of the whole person, but in the present state of psychology such comments would be subject to considerable qualifications and limitations. The subsequent chapters in this book deal with the psychological approach to religion so it is unnecessary to make further comment at this point. The study begins in the next chapter with a discussion of how psychologists investigate religion.

SUMMARY

It has not been the intention of this chapter to provide a systematic overview of the various studies of religion. The main purpose has been to provide the reader with a picture which will enable him to fit psychological studies within an overall framework of a multi-discipline approach to the problem of religion. To that end the contributions of history, anthropology, sociology, philosophy and theology have been considered.

In chapter 2 it was stated that psychology was concerned with the origin, development, and maintenance of an individual's religion. There are a number of problems which arise when an attempt is made to study religion in this way. It is therefore necessary to consider these problems before examining the way psychology investigates religion.

PROBLEMS OF THE STUDY

One of the first difficulties that the psychologist faces is the problem of objectivity. Objectivity in any scientific investigation is essential. This presents few obstacles when only the collection of facts is involved. It is the interpretation of facts and in the construction of theories that the importance of objectivity has not been given its rightful place, thus possibly hindering scientific development. Certainly maintaining objectivity can be difficult. Sometimes investigators become so emotionally involved in a theory which they have constructed or adopted that they either turn a blind eye to facts which contradict it, or delay conducting the crucial test for their theory. It seems that when scientists are concerned with religious phenomena this emotional involvement is at its height. Perhaps such involvement is unavoidable if a personal judgment about religion has already been made. In such cases it is almost impossible not to arrive at an interpretation of the facts which is coloured by that previous judgment. There is another side to the problem. Geddes MacGregor (1960) wants more than objectivity in the study of religion. He calls for ' existential ' thinking as well as scientific thought about religion. By existential he means ' thinking not in detachment from a situation but in involvement with it ' (ibid., p. 18). He is suggesting that someone who is personally involved in religion can see factors which may be missed by a person outside the situation; so he claims that both scientific and existential thought are important in the study of religious behaviour.

Existential philosophy has found a place in psychology and its significance is increasing. Often it is referred to as a 'third force', joining behaviourism and psychoanalysis as the greatest influences on psychology. Well-known psychologists such as Allport, Maslow, Mowrer and Laing have been responsible for applying this philosophical approach to the psychological study of man.

Existential psychology is an approach or viewpoint which stresses man as a unique individual, a uniqueness which can never be totally explained by physical theories or psychological models of a behaviouristic or psychoanalytical type. Existential psychology seeks to complement all the other approaches to man and thus provide a comprehensive picture of the whole man as he really exists. It is concerned essentially with the problems of individuals and less with the laws or rules which are applicable to man in general. Understanding man in his entirety is the basic motivation of the existential approach. The problems it deals with are those which psychology in general has ignored, such as freedom and responsibility, death, suffering and the meaning of life. It attempts to explore consciousness and inner feelings.

It has long been recognised that psychology lacks an all-embracing, theoretical framework or approach on which to hang all its empirical evidence, and thus produce a meaningful picture. Existential psychology may be an attempt to bring such meaning and purpose to psychological research, but as yet it does not appear to have been effectively applied to the psychology of religion.

Most of the study has been devoted to psychopathology, although Allport (1955) does discuss religion in terms of the development of personality. The basic concept is the idea of becoming. For the normal child 'the foundations of character were established by the age of three or five only in the sense that he is now free to become; he is not retarded; he is well launched on the course of continuous and unimpeded growth' (ibid., p. 33). Religious belief and experience form an integral part of becoming even the ultimate goal of the process – enabling the individual to relate meaningfully to creation. 'While religion certainly fortifies the individual against the inroads of anxiety, doubt and despair, it also provides the forward intention that enables him at each stage of his becoming to relate himself fully to the totality of being' (ibid., p. 96).

The character of religious belief raises another difficulty; for such beliefs are not only a cognitive response to a given set of propositions, they also involve an emotional response; this arises because of the very nature of the propositions themselves. They are generally beyond proof, or disproof, and therefore the tenacity and intensity with which the beliefs are held may be increased in order to compensate for the absence of any logical proof. This is confirmed by Thouless (1935), who found that the intensity of agreement, or disagreement, with religious propositions was much higher than that for propositions of fact. It seems that intensity and truth are highly correlated in the mind of the religious man when he considers his religious beliefs. It can therefore be seen that for the religious person the relationship between truth, and what he believes, can be one of almost complete correspondence. In psychology it is assumed that beliefs, no matter with what intensity they are held, need have no direct relationship with truth. It is this problem of truth which has led to a questioning of just how far psychological advance affects religious truth.

Undoubtedly religious behaviour is a legitimate study for psychology, but the questions psychology cannot answer concern the truth and value of religion. Such questions are outside the scope of scientific enquiry. Religious people can legitimately claim that any psychological explanations of religious behaviour merely indicate God's methods of revealing Himself to man, whereas the non-religious man could conclude that the scientific findings were the only necessary explanation. Both may hold to their opinion for neither can be proved or disproved. Despite scientific advances the central problem of truth remains unresolved.

Both the limitations and benefits of psychology in relation to religion are apparent. It can study the actual behaviour of religious people, how they become and how they remain religious. What it cannot do is to say whether the particular ideas of religion are true or false. It can, however, provide alternative explanations for the existence of religious ideas and religious behaviour, and in this way challenge their validity. It can also uncover facts which might put religion in an unfavourable light – if for instance it was found that all religious people were neurotic. But a pragmatic assessment of religion would examine the significance and value religion has for the individual, at the present moment, not how, or even why, such beliefs and behaviour were adopted. Psychology can assist religion by indicating just how people become religious, and this information may be used in the propagation of religion. It can also clarify the effects that religion has on other aspects of behaviour, moral behaviour perhaps, which might help in alleviating certain social problems (such as alcoholism).

Another significant difficulty involves the problem of language. Theology and psychology have different technical languages. Many terms used in one do not appear in the other, and in many cases there are no obvious equivalents. But perhaps the greatest confusion occurs where the same word is used in both languages but with a different meaning or different emphasis. There are a number of examples which come to mind. The word 'dependence' in psychology has a somewhat negative loading, implying emotional immaturity, inadequacy, and the need for support from others. In theology this same word has a positive loading, especially when applied to the relationship between the individual and his God : it speaks of a realisation of creaturely dependence on the Creator, and a reliance on God's providence in life and death. Adherence to a certain set of beliefs may be described in psychology as 'rigidity' if they are held in a dogmatic and inflexible way, but in theology such adherence may be described as steadfastness. In the former case, rigidity implies a type of person who is set in his ways and unable to adapt to changing circumstances : while in the latter case, steadfastness may be used to describe a person who suffers a martyr's death rather than deny his faith. One we denigrate, the other we admire. In the MMPI (Minnesota Multiphasic Personality Inventory) a certain set of responses, e.g. I am very religious (more than most people), form a scale labelled 'Pharisaic Virtue', while in religious circles this same set of reponses may be considered 'thinking soberly', and seen as a sign of true and not false humility.

This cursory examination of the difficulties of language leads to a deeper philosophical problem associated with the meaning and use of religious language. The suggested solution to this problem is to consider religious language as analogical. To adopt any other interpretation implies that nothing can be said about the divine when using human language. If all religious language is analogical, then a further problem for the investigating psychologist considering a religious concept, is that of finding the 'point' of a particular analogy. Most people realise that when the religious man talks about God as Father, in the main he does not mean a human being of the male sex, but merely implies that there are certain similarities of care and protection common to both God and a human father. It is in this respect that Freud's theory (1927) that God is a fantasy father figure is inadequate. Finding this inadequacy is not to deny that for some people this is all God is, but to draw attention to the fact that for the vast majority of religious people God is not regarded as a human father figure, but only resembles a father in certain given and highly qualified ways. Therefore, the psychologist needs to be sure of what is generally understood by a given religious concept before drawing conclusions about its significance in religious behaviour.

Another concept which has produced similar confusion concerns the view of the Church as the ' bride ' of Christ. The deep significance that the monastic orders attach to this concept may be the source of the sexual symbolism which seems to be characteristic of the writings of many of the mystics (Leuba 1925 and Thouless 1924); and their sexual abstinence probably only contributes to the frequency with which such symbolism accurs.

DEFINING RELIGIOUS BEHAVIOUR

The next problem to be considered requires some attempt to define the word religion, or more precisely in a psychological context, religious belief and behaviour. It would be helpful to know by virtue of what quality a given activity is denoted as religious, as opposed to non-religious or irreligious, but there is no easy answer to this question. There seems to be as many definitions of religion as there are of personality. William James (1902) for the purpose of his book on religious experience, distinguishes between institutional religion and personal religion. The former it concerned with ' theology, ceremony and ecclesiastical organisation ', the latter with ' the inner disposition of man himself, his conscience, his deserts, his helplessness, his incompleteness '. While this is a very useful distinction, it is necessary also to attend to other factors – such as the reactions, the attitudes, and the general behaviour of the individual in relation to the religious institution and its associated behaviour patterns. James recognised this aspect of personal religion but thinks of it as secondary because his method of investigation utilises the extremes of religious experience, which are in the main outside of institutional religion.

The suggestion is, then, that the area covered by the psychological study of religion will be concerned mainly with the individual, his behaviour in respect of the religious group to which he belongs and his behaviour in the relationship he has formed with what he thinks of as divine, or treats as divine. The definition is not meant to be exact or exhaustive. Its purpose is merely to draw a rough boundary to mark the limits of psychological research. It is possible to add to the above study the behaviour of the religious community as a group and thus extend the sphere of interest into the realm of sociology. It is obvious that the behaviour of the group is an important factor in a true picture of religious phenomena, but in most psychological investigations the group activity will be subsidiary to the individual behaviour.

Having in some sense delineated the possible area of psychological investigation, it is necessary to decide what exactly constitutes *religious behaviour*. As James (1902) pointed out, the behaviour that takes place in a religious situation is not behaviour which is unknown in a non-religious setting. It is not the behaviour itself which designates it as religious, 'but the object to which it is directed, and the purpose for which it is undertaken'. James observes 'religious love is only man's natural emotion of love directed to a religious object, religious fear is only the ordinary fear of commerce, so to speak, the common quaking of the human breast in so far as the notion of divine retribution may arouse it' (ibid., p. 27). There are striking resemblances between primitive war dances and the contemporary pop scene, but the object and purpose are quite different – as can be deduced from subsequent behaviour.

It follows that activities normally referred to as religious, might not be deemed as such if the purpose for which they were effected were taken into consideration. One cannot always gauge religious commitment and belief simply through observance of people engaging in institutional ceremonies. For example many baptisms are simply social gatherings, 'the wetting of the baby's head', containing little religious significance or worship. These observations illustrate the complexity of the subject when there is a change from assessing objective overt behaviour to a consideration of the essentially subjective concept of internal motivation in trying to understand the term 'religious'. In order to avoid such subjective considerations it is necessary to confine investigations to behaviour, like prayer, which by its very nature is 'obviously' religious. It must be borne in mind, however, that every individual who participates in the group activity may not be behaving in a religious manner. In order to sort out the sheep from the goats a value judgment will be made on the part of the investigator which may well lack scientific validity. Thus one is faced with a difficult problem, either to restrict research to the objective and classify all who take part ostensibly in religious behaviour as in some sense religious, and then, (1) investigate types of religious people, or, (2) to make judgments about a person's religious behaviour at a subjective level. The latter is almost impossible in any scientific investigation, and so investigators have turned to the former as being the more fruitful. In the context of this procedure Argyle (1958) has made the useful suggestion that a fundamental distinction should be made between the 'genuinely devout' and the 'conventionally religious ', who presumably just go through the motions of religious activity, like the ' head wetters ' !

In previous research certain claims have been made about the character of religious people, but little account, if any, has been taken of the *content* of their beliefs. If any distinction was made between differences in religious beliefs it was normally related to denominational differences. In the author's experience it would appear that significant differences in this area are to a great extent independent of denominational allegiance. It is important to find out whether these differences are associated with differences in personality : whether the ritualist is of a particular personality type and the evangelist of a different personality, or whether these differences are merely the result of learning. In fact it is useful to know to what extent personality affects the religious beliefs a person holds. Obviously the answers to a number of these questions are relevant outside the psychological field. If differences in belief and practice arise in some way as the result of differences in personality, then the realisation of this might encourage the ongoing attempts towards Christian unity. Beliefs and differences in belief have already been mentioned, but a further topic of interest is the relationship between belief and behaviour. Spinks (1960) distinguishes three meanings of the word belief : (1) belief as a noun, indicating what we believe; (2) belief as assent, accepting a proposition as correct; and (3) belief as commitment to some particular issue. Only the second and third meanings are important for they are most useful in helping to assess the relationship between belief and behaviour. They indicate the theological distinction between belief and faith and the difference between belief and attitude as usually defined by psychologists.

When the religious belief is no more than a cognitive assent to a given proposition it is not expected that it will result in any corresponding religious action. However, when a belief is internalised it comes in the third category, belief as commitment, when a change in behaviour is necessarily involved. Belief in this sense has a motivational factor associated with it. Most religious beliefs do influence the way a person acts, especially in the case of the genuinely devout, who are classed as such because their beliefs are so evident in their overt behaviour. A fairly reliable indication of the type of behaviour a person is likely to display is found by examining his attitudes and beliefs. It is more practical to obtain a sample of an individual's attitudes by questionnaire than by prolonged and detailed observation.

THE STUDY OF RELIGION

In any scientific investigation a method of analysis must be chosen which is appropriate for the behaviour under examination. This is important because the method of analysis affects the way in which the data is collected. There are two main methods, the idiographic or case study method and the nomothetic approach.

Idiographic Approaches

By this method as much information as possible is collected about a person, and hypotheses are made to try to explain the mechanism underlying the person's beliefs, attitudes, and other characteristics. Investigators, many of whom are clinical psychologists, who support this method feel that causation is a complicated process which is not revealed by the discovery of significant correlation coefficients between personality factors, but only by a detailed investigation of the individual. They also maintain that insufficient weight is given to the various processes that may operate in people to produce a similar score on a test. Whilst this fact is admitted, the whole basis of statistical psychology is founded on the reasonable assumption that individuals are not all unique and different in every conceivable way, but fall into certain broad groups and that individuality comprises the unique combination of groups to which a person belongs.

There are advantages in the idiographic approach. An elaborate and carefully annotated collection of data on one individual may provide information about the complex interaction of variables which would be beyond the scope of normal nomothetic comparisons. Smith et al (1956) emphasised this point when they investigated at great depth the complex interplay of attitude and personality variables. Their study was confined to a small number of individuals but indicated the great wealth of information available when this method is used. Existentialist psychologists feel that the idiographic approach is the best method for understanding man as a complete individual. It provides information about what he sees as meaningful and purposeful in his life. New techniques in this approach, such as Kelly's Repertory Grid test, have added sophistication and greater scientific acceptability to the method.

Nomothetic Approaches

In this method a fairly large number of people are evaluated on a number of psychological tests measuring personality traits, usually by means of questionnaires in the case of religious beliefs. Statistical methods then enable the investigator to explore the relationships between the various traits and to determine the possible causal agents and the direction in which they may be operating. This intensive statistical treatment can produce reasonably reliable predictions which can be tested. Similar predictions are not so readily available nor so easily tested when the case-study method is used.

One of the main problems arising from statistical analysis concerns the direction of causality. Does A cause B or B cause A or does a third variable C cause both A and B? There is no simple answer to such a problem; any conclusions that are made must be tentative. There are, however, certain common-sense factors which maye be used to determine the direction of causation. When variables are independent of time, like sex, these are more likely to be causal variables or at least related to causal variables. In addition we may conclude that when two variables are significantly correlated and one occurs in time before the other, then the first is either itself the causal variable or is directly related to it. We are able to make such a conclusion because we do not believe that a cause can work backwards in time. If we accept that causal variables precede dependent variables in time then we can design longitudinal studies, lasting many years, which can determine the sequence of events and variable occurrences making it possible to determine causal factors. The disadvantage of longitudinal or long-term studies is that they are expensive, difficult to maintain, and not an effective method for studying every type of variable. This means it is often necessary to infer the direction of causality from short-term experiments. In such cases the results should be treated with extreme caution and further experiments carried out before any firm conclusions are reached. If such caution is observed then the nomothetic approach does provide the most effective and systematic means of exploring religious behaviour.

The nomothetic approach to psychological investigation can be divided into three sub-categories, laboratory experiments, field studies and questionnaire methods.

Laboratory Experiments. In a laboratory we produce a controlled environment in which only one variable is changed and the consequent effects observed and recorded; it is essentially the application of laboratory techniques to psychological problems. In general, laboratory experiments are more easily applied to psycho-

B

logical investigation, when physiological measurements can be made – reaction time, galvanic skin response, pupil dilation, etc. – although attempts to investigate more complex human behaviour in a laboratory setting are increasing, for example the affects of stress on human behaviour.

Field Studies. Field studies utilise observational techniques. A detailed record of the behaviour of an animal, or a human, or a group, is kept for a given period of time. This provides information about the character, frequency and duration of certain specific behaviour patterns which are common to the individual being studied. Field study methods are widely used in animal psychology, anthropology, cross-cultural comparisons of human behaviour, and in any situation where it is necessary to study the individual or the group in its natural surroundings. The advantage of this method is that it avoids the artificial atmosphere of the laboratory and provided the individual or group is not conscious of the experimenter, we have a record of behaviour in a perfectly natural environment. The basic disadvantage is that the observer has no control over the situation and thus can only make tentative suggestions about the most important variables contributing to a particular behavioural event. Wherever possible subjects should be studied both in their natural surroundings and under laboratory conditions.

There are two refinements to the basic field study method, natural experiments and field experiments. A natural experiment occurs when during normal field observation, an unsolicited and unexpected variable is introduced into the situation and the experimenter is able to record the change in behaviour which the introduction of the new variable may have caused. If, during an experimenter's observation of crowd behaviour at a football match, the referee was struck by lightning (perhaps an answer to prayer!) and he was able to observe the consequent behaviour of the crowd and players then this would constitute a natural experiment.

The field experiment is very similar to the natural experiment except that the experimenter is directly responsible for introducing the new stimulus. If, for example, the experimenter introduced a stuffed animal into the normal environment of a group of monkeys and recorded the way the monkeys responded to the stuffed animal, this would be described as a field experiment (cf. Harlow's work (1959) using mother-surrogates to investigate the behaviour of infant monkeys).

Questionnaire Methods. The questionnaire method is one in which we ask a number of individuals to answer a series of questions. There are two basic types – survey questionnaires and personality assessment questionnaires. The former is mainly concerned with collecting information about the activities and the likes and dislikes of the individuals answering the questions. Opinion polls and market research make wide use of this type of questionnaire. It is very important in surveys that the individuals are encouraged to answer truthfully; if they do not the results may be invalid. Personality assessment questionnaires are somewhat different, the main concern here being the investigation of the underlying personality structures which determine an individual's response to a given question or set of questions. The way this is done is to compare the individual's answer pattern as revealed by the questionnaire with the answer pattern of a number of standardised groups. The more closely the individual's pattern follows that of a particular group the more likely it is that he belongs to that group. For example, if diagnosed neurotics form one of the standardised groups and the individual's pattern is very similar to the pattern of that group, then we can conclude that he too is a neurotic. The greater the similarity between the individual's answer profile and that of the standard group, the greater the probability that the individual has the same characteristics as the group.

These are some of the general research methods that are used in psychology, but not all are equally applicable to the investigation of religious behaviour. It is extremely difficult, for instance, to use laboratory methods to investigate religious behaviour, as this sort of behaviour is dependent on its environmental setting. The other three methods may be applied. The case study technique is useful in investigating the origin and development of religious beliefs in a particular individual. Case study methods can be extended to include library investigation where the biographies or autobiographies of religious leaders – St. Paul or Charles Wesley, for example – or other religious people are examined for information about the origin and development of their religious experiences.

The field study method employed by anthropologists provides useful information about the growth of religion within the general development of mankind. Cross-cultural studies enable us to compare and contrast the religious behaviour and belief of various races and cultures.

The natural experiment is important in the investigation of

religious behaviour; for example an investigator may be able to observe sudden conversion taking place during evangelistic meetings.

By far the most important research tool in the investigation of religious behaviour is the questionnaire. Both types of questionnaire are important; the survey method gives us information about church attendance, denominational allegiance, age of conversion, regularity of private prayer and Bible reading, etc.; while the personality assessment questionnaire provides information about the subject's personality characteristics and the religious attitudes he holds.

These three research methods have been the tools most frequently used for the psychological investigation of religious behaviour.

Measuring religious belief or behaviour has always presented some difficulty. Questionnaires of one sort or another have been used most frequently, but two more recent research techniques, the semantic differential and the Q sort, are now being used for investigating religious behaviour.

Semantic Differential

The semantic differential is an attempt to analyse the psychological meaning of words. It is concerned with the conative or affective component of meaning. The technique employed requires the subject to rate a word on a series of seven point scales of bipolar adjectives. For example, the subject may be asked to rate the word God on the good–bad or strong–weak scales. Osgood, who developed the technique, has found three basic factors or dimensions of affective meaning which he has named evaluation (good–bad; beautiful–ugly, etc.), activity (active–passive; fast–slow, etc.), and potency (strong–weak; large–small, etc.). In choosing the bipolar adjectives one is going to use, it is probably wise to ensure representation from each of these factors. The starting point in the application of the semantic differential is choosing the words or concepts relevant to the problem being investigated; then one has to decide which rating scales to use and how many are required.

This technique has proved a very useful tool in the cognitive analysis of beliefs. It furnishes valuable information about what is understood by such religious concepts as God, forgiveness, salvation, etc. In this way it has brought certain subjective aspects of religious behaviour that have usually been difficult, if not impossible to examine, within the scope of scientific analysis.

Q Methodology

The Q methodology is another useful research technique that has been developed recently. It provides correlation between persons or clusters of persons rather than between tests as in the usual correlation procedure. It makes wide use of factor analysis and analysis of variance and sophistication in these statistical procedures is necessary for the productive application of Q methodology. The basic procedure of the technique is the Q sort. This involves ranking a number of statements (usually between 60–120) on a given subject according to some given criterion, for example, the extent to which the individual approves or disapproves of the statement. It would be extremely difficult and time consuming to attempt a simple ranking task, so usually a modified ranking procedure is followed. The statements are typed on cards and the cards sorted into (usually) eleven piles, each one representing a discrete step between approval and disapproval. It is also usual for a forced sort to be used, in which case a fixed number of cards is allowed for each pile. The number allowed is normally calculated so as to produce a normal distribution, the largest number at the centre, the smallest at the extremes of the range. The forced sort has the advantage of simplifying the necessary statistical treatment of the results. Q methodology has a limited application, and it is not readily applicable to large random samples. Essentially it is a tool which can be used to explore and identify factors and their interrelation in relatively new areas of research or to examine in detail established findings. It is principally a heuristic technique.

THE RELIGIOUS CLIMATE IN THE WEST

A further difficulty that the investigating psychologist has to face is the varying support for organised religions. Many of the measures of religious behaviour that he uses may be subject to modification by changes in the relative attractiveness or fashionableness of religion. Thus comparison of results obtained at different times may be difficult to interpret. With the decline in the established and organised Churches of Britain, and to a lesser extent of America, there seems to be an increase in the following of Eastern religions. This may simply be a consequence of the greater contact that these cultures now have with Eastern faiths, through increased immigration and the mass media, or it may represent a dissatisfaction with the traditional approaches to life and a search for new and stimulating experiences. The increasing use of drugs may also be indicative of a similar attitude. These changes need to be explored in depth, for they could provide valuable information about the underlying motives which encourage the development of religious belief.

SUMMARY

In this chapter some of the problems associated with the investigation of religious phenomena have been examined. The scope and subject of the psychology of religion has also been reviewed. Then followed an explanation of the meaning of religious behaviour and religious beliefs and the relationship between the two.

Finally we reviewed the research methods used by psychologists and discussed the relevance of these methods for investigating religious behaviour.

4

Variables of Religious Belief and
Behaviour

Part I: Classifications

There are numerous variables associated with religion (see Dittes
1969) and many have been used by investigators in an attempt
to measure different aspects of religious belief and behaviour.
However some of the variables are not amenable to the more
usual methods of measurement such as interval or ordinal measurement. Often the experimenter can only classify the material into
mutually exclusive categories, which is normally referred to as
nominal measurement. There are three important variables of this
type which have considerable significance in the study of religious
behaviour, religion, denomination and religious conversion. The
first two are concerned with membership while the third deals
with the origin of the individual's belief. Religious people can be
classified in terms of the religion they follow and the denomination
to which they belong. Denomination is usually applied to the
Christian faith, but most world religions have their distinctive
variants.

RELIGIONS

An examination of the classification by religion reveals the relative
dearth of material of a comparative nature. There is a tendency
in the psychology of religion to restrict investigations to the
Judaeo-Christian faiths neglecting a great percentage of the
world population who follow some other creed. There are two
main reasons for this. In the first place modern experimental
psychology is Western in origin, it therefore tends to investigate
its own culture which is predominantly Judaeo-Christian. In the
second place experimental investigations require individuals who
are willing to be subjects in a research project. Until quite recently
people of non-Christian faiths were not readily available in
sufficient numbers to merit scientific investigation. The greater
contact between East and West is helping to bring the other world
religions under the psychological microscope. There is a con-

tinuing development of psychology in India, Japan and other Eastern countries which means that the religious beliefs of people living in these countries are now being investigated. In addition there are fairly large groups of individuals now resident in America and Europe who are devotees of Eastern religious beliefs. Such people could be used as subjects for research in the psychology of religion and indeed some of their number can be expected to become psychological investigators themselves. There seems little need to justify the necessity of investigating religions other than the Judaeo-Christian group. Christianity, while it is the largest religion numerically, only forms about a third of the world population. Table 1 gives an estimate of the numerical size of some of the world religions. There is considerable difficulty in estimating the size of religions, especially since the national commitment of China and Japan to religion has been politically overruled. Similarly it is difficult to estimate Marxist following. In addition there is the ever present problem of determining nominal and actual commitment.

TABLE I : ESTIMATES OF THE MEMBERSHIP OF SOME WORLD RELIGIONS

Religion	Estimated numbers in millions
Christianity	
Roman Catholic	518
Protestant	316
Eastern Orthodox	130
	1,027
Buddhism	168
Hinduism	420
Islam	465

(abstracted from *The Readers Digest Great World Atlas* 1972)

Despite the millions of people committed to religions other than Christianity, psychological investigations of them have been very limited. Many are at the descriptive level, comparing and contrasting the beliefs and practices of one religion with another or comparing their underlying philosophies. There is, however, evidence that with the development of interest in the area this gap in the psychology of religion will soon be filled. Some investigations deserve mention and indicate the direction that research of this kind is taking.

Most studies are searching for differences between members of different religions. For example Ray-Chowdhury (1958) made an extremely useful comparison between Hindu and Moslem women at an Indian college. He used an experimental version of the Allport-Vernon-Lindsay Study of Values and found significant differences between the two groups of women on social, political and religious values. Moslems were more interested in religion; Hindus more interested in social and political values. He concluded that the socio-cultural pattern of the Hindus represented in the group were much closer to the Anglo-American pattern than that produced by the Moslem women.

Meredith (1959) compared Buddhist and Protestant women. He used an adjective-checking method of self-description to investigate possible differences between Japanese-American college women with Buddhist religious beliefs and similar women with Protestant religious beliefs. He found that a significantly larger number of Budhhists described themselves as excitable, pleasure-seeking, irritable, and stubborn than the Protestants, while universally a larger number described themselves as religious. How useful this approach is depends on the validity of the adjective-checking method. Meredith suggests that further work is necessary in this area.

A number of investigators have been concerned with determining the influence of the various religions on other activities or attitudes. Sometimes significant differences are found. For example, people from different religious backgrounds seem to differ in respect of the kind of stimulation they seek from their environment. Zuckerman et al. (1964) have developed what they have called a Sensation-Seeking Scale. The scale was used by Berkowitz (1967) to compare American students, Thai students, and Buddhist monks. It was found that American students gain the highest score on the scale and the monks the lowest, while the Thai students score fell between the score of the other two groups. This result corresponds with Berkowitz's prediction which was based on the assumption of the influence of Buddhist teachings calling for a renounciation of a great deal of worldly excitement. The Buddhist culture permeates the Thai nation, but would be unlikely to be adhered to quite so strictly as by the Buddhist monks.

Sometimes, however, religion seems to play a less important role. A comparison of the attitudes of Christian and Moslem Lebanese villagers were examined by means of interviews. There was little evidence that religious differences produced any significant contrasts in basic attitudes. Fetter (1964) suggest that economic and geographical differences are more significant in village life than differences in religious beliefs.

An interesting attempt has also been made to see if religion influences biological or genetic factors. Schull et al. (1962) compared Buddhist and Roman Catholics living in the Japanese Island of Kuroshima. Differences were found on reproductive performance, frequency of visual handicap and abnormal colour perception, and A,B,C, blood group distribution frequencies. The main interest of the investigators was to determine whether religious beliefs influenced the biology of the group over the years. It was difficult to demonstrate that such biological differences as existed were attributable to religious beliefs because not all the population had a common background.

As already indicated, much of the literature on this subject points out similarities between certain religious rituals and beliefs. Some authors have drawn attention to similarities between religious beliefs and psychological disciplines, especially psychoanalysis and hypnosis. The research work that has been quoted above indicates a number of similarities between Eastern and Western religious belief and behaviour and their correlates, but considerably more research work is necessary before a clear picture of this section of the psychology of religion becomes available.

DENOMINATIONS

The research using the classification of Christian denomination is much more extensive, as there have been many attempts to compare the religious behaviour and belief of members of different denominations. Indeed most research uses a multidenominational sample and therefore in many cases comparisons can be drawn between the results for each denomination taking part.

Much American research in this area divides the religious population into three groups. Protestant, Catholic and Jew, while the division in England is, Church of England, Catholic and Nonconformist.

There has always been an interest in the comparative intelligence of the various denominations. Fry (1933) produced a scale based on denominational over-representation in *Who's Who*; this list is very similar to that compiled by Pratt (1937) which was derived from intelligence test results of a student population. They both favour Unitarians, Episcopalians and Congregationalists as the most intelligent, while Catholics, Lutherans and Methodists are lowest on the scale.

Political attitudes of individuals from different denominations produce interesting results. Most voting statistics indicate that Protestants are the most conservative, but according to Sappenfield (1942) Roman Catholics are more conservative on Political Attitude Scales. One possible explanation is based on the class composition of the two groups, but Lazarsfield (1944) found that American Protestants are more Republican even when social class is held constant. The solution would seem to lie in the social setting, the voting behaviour of Roman Catholics is linked with their status as an immigrant minority group, rather than with their political attitudes. The investigations of Lipset et al. (1954) confirm this tendency. It was shown that many members of religious denominations which form minority groups in the general population tend to support the more radical parties.

Slater (1947) analysed the denominational percentages of Army breakdowns in an English hospital during World War II. His findings indicated a slightly higher rate of neurosis for religious people, especially for Jews. Jews of course were subjected to additional stress during the war and this might account for the result.

A number of investigators have been interested in the appeal of the denomination to different social classes. Pope (1948) analysed the social class composition of Protestants and Roman Catholics, and found that there was a greater proportion of higher class individuals among the Protestants. This contrast between Protestants and Catholics was not found before 1939. It seems that considerable change must have taken place during World War II probably as a consequence of immigration from Roman Catholic countries. Weber's (1905) suggestion that the Protestant ethic is important in the development of capitalism may influence the class composition of Protestant and Roman Catholic groups, but Pope's findings indicate the importance of other factors.

Knapp and Goodrich (1951), using Weber's theoretical framework, discovered that a high proportion of successful scientists came from American Liberal Arts colleges and that comparatively few came from Roman Catholic universities. They suggest that the Protestant ideology is more conducive to scientific research.

Sometimes it is social class and not religious belief that may be responsible for certain findings. It is necessary to pay close attention to such factors when interpreting experimental results. Occasionally it is possible to discover whether class or religion is the most significant influence. For example, Trenaman (1952) when examining the statistics for delinquency found that Roman Catholics had a higher percentage of delinquency than other denominations in Britain. They noted that this could not be explained by class differences because Nonconformist Churches had a similar class composition but had the least percentage of delinquents. Class differences may not be significant in this situation, but differences in national origin may be important, in the light of Pope's findings.

It is interesting to contemplate whether the various denominational belief systems influence attitude and behaviour in different ways. It is possible that a person's attitude to his belief system influences the extent to which it modifies his behaviour. There do appear to be some denominational differences. London et al. (1964) attempted to get some estimate of how Roman Catholic, Protestant and Jewish students perceive their own faith. He found that Jews portrayed their faith as more liberal in terms of doctrine than did either Catholics or Protestants. The Protestants in turn had a more liberal evaluation of their creed than the Catholics. There were no significant differences between the groups for guilt feelings or ethical standards of conduct, but they all thought that their official creeds were more restrictive than they need be. There is little doubt that denominational belief does have a significant effect on other atittudes. For example a group of religious people belonging to the Baptist, Catholic, Christian Church of Christ, Episcopalian, Lutheran, Methodist, Missionary Baptist, Presbyterian and Unitarian denominations were asked by Pang (1968) to complete a questionnaire purporting to measure altruism, conformity, fundamentalism, mysticism and superstition. An analysis of variance indicated that denominations are significantly different from one another on all measures at a probability level of .05 or better.

Prejudice is not only a significant variable among religious people as a whole but also between denominations. Parry (1949) found that non-churchgoing Protestants were more anti-semitic than Protestants who attend church, while Roman Catholics were the least anti-semitic of the three groups. Hoppe (1969) suggested that there is greater affinity between Catholics and Jews because they share a minority group status. Allport (1954) again found the quality of religious belief an important variable in prejudice. He found that a group of fervent Roman Catholics were less prejudiced than a group of more conventionally religious Catholics.

Closely associated with the concept of prejudice is the idea of an authoritarian personality. Most research indicates some denominational differences especially between Roman Catholics and Protestants. If these findings are valid we should expect certain differences between these two groups in their willingness to accept others. Long (1965) found that Catholics showed a greater acceptance of other people than Protestants. This is somewhat unexpected for Roman Catholics seems to gain higher authoritarian scores, and as authoritarianism has been linked to intolerance then the opposite finding might have been anticipated. Long suggested that the stress Protestants put on individualism and the Roman Catholics' stress on corporativeness and group mindedness may be the reasons for the result.

Arguments can be put forward for making a link between authoritarianism and the way people deal with frustration. Reaction to frustration also seems to produce denominational differences. A group of Baptist, Roman Catholic and Jewish children were asked to complete the Rosenzweig Picture-Frustration Study by Kirschner et al. (1962). They found that Jews tended to be more extrapunitive but less intropunitive than the other two denominational groups; while Catholics were more concerned with Obstacle-Dominance. Brown (1965) also used the Rosenzweig Picture-Frustration Study to test a hypothesis put forward by Argyle (1958), who had suggested that Roman Catholics are extrapunitive and Protestants intropunitive. Brown does provide general support for the extrapunitiveness of Roman Catholics but the assertions about the intropunitiveness of Protestants is only confirmed by the females of the sample. He also points out that Protestants are such a heterogeneous group that comparisons with Roman Catholics should be made only in terms of denominational groupings or some similar criterion.

Sutker, Sutker and Kilpatrick (1970), investigated the effects of religious affiliation on sexual attitudes. They report only limited support for their prediction of significant differences among Southern religious denominations. Differences were normally seen within each sex category and related to distinctions between the religious individual and the non-religious reference group. They conclude that in terms of sexual attitudes and behaviour, Southern Protestants, Catholics and Jews form a rather homogenous group.

Religious belief not only affects attitudes but behaviour. Dice et al. (1965) examined a random sample of the population of Ann Arbor. An analysis of the behaviour of the major denominations indicated that the Roman Catholics attended church more than twice as often as Protestants, who in turn attended church more than twice as often as those without church affiliation. They found no differences in terms of differential fertility among the major denominations and suggested that this might be because of the similarities of education, occupation and custom. The implication is that family size is not determined by religious belief but more by social and economic factors. This explanation may be applicable to situations in Britain. Most denominations have been declining in recent years but the Roman Catholic church has been growing. Lenski (1953, and unpublished work quoted by Argyle in 1958) studying this phenomenon found that it is the high birth rate, and immigration of Roman Catholics, rather than evangelism which has produced the growth. As Pope's (1948) work would indicate, it is usually the lower class Catholics which form the bulk of the immigrants. Sociological studies of religion have made wide use of the denominational classification as it has proved a very useful method of investigating the sociological factors associated with religion. The importance of denominational allegiance in this area will become apparent when the sociological factors are discussed in chapter 8. One cautionary note about using denomination as a variable of religious belief is sounded by Thouless (1954) who examined intra-denominational differences and concluded that the great differences between members in one denomination may result in people from different denominations showing greater similarity in belief and practise. Ranck (1955) suggested that differences in denominational adherence reflect differing religious orientation. He preferred to divide his religious sample into liberals and conservatives depending on the content of their religious views.

Most of the work we have examined in this section does provide significant differences between denominations, but many results are contradictory and so cast doubt on the usefulness of denominational allegiance as a valid and reliable measure. It has been pointed out that the Protestant category is a very heterogeneous group, and even single Protestant denominations have shown considerable intra-group variations in terms of fundamentalism and ritual. These facts also indicate the difficulties of studying religious behaviour from a denominational point of view.

Recent developments in the Roman Catholic Church may also indicate that it is a less homogeneous group than originally thought. There certainly seems to be a significant difference of opinion over birth control and the place of personal responsibility and church discipline in decision making.

CONVERSION TYPES

There are many situations which influence the development of religious belief, the attitude of the parents, childhood experiences, the mass media, etc. – each may play an important part. It can be argued that almost any experience can have religious significance for an individual and therefore systematic analysis is extremely difficult. What is perhaps more important is, not so much the kind of experiences but the way they integrate and cohere together to produce some sort of religious commitment. This phenomenon leads us to a consideration of conversion type and the experimental work done on the subject. But before considering the various types of conversion experience it is necessary to examine the topic as a whole.

The phenomenon of religious conversion has aroused considerable interest over the years, especially conversions of a sudden and dramatic character. To a large extent this type of conversion, normally referred to as a sudden conversion, occurs during religious meetings of a missionary or revivalistic nature. Often such conversions are accompanied by hysterical manifestations, and this is one of the main reasons why they have attracted attention. Davenport (1905) in his investigation of religious revivals draws attention to the spectacular. He reported that revivals were often scenes of great drama, with people speaking in tongues, barking, jerking and twitching, while others collapsed and lay on the ground. Pratt (1924) suggests that evangelists like John Wesley preached in order to arouse great anxiety in their audience. Such techniques might explain to some extent the highly emotional and hysterical scenes reported by Davenport.

Coe (1916) in his book 'The Psychology of Religion' reports on a study he made of 100 religious converts. He found that those in the group who had experienced a sudden conversion were more likely to produce motor automatism during hypnosis. The implication from this is that conversion experience may be linked with personality characteristics, and that subjects with an hysterical personality trait may be more susceptible to sudden conversion. The more mundane aspects of conversion are discussed by Clark (1928). He examined in detail the relation of conversion to age, attendance at Sunday school, suffering from a sense of sin, etc.

The evangelistic efforts of Billy Graham and his team provide a chance to investigate more recent sudden conversions. Colquhoun (1965) provides numerous statistics of the campaigns held in Britain in 1954 and 1955. For example the ratio of male-female conversions was 1 : 1.8 and the average age of conversion was 15 years, but about 40 per cent were converted at 19 years or over. To make valid comparisons however it is necessary to determine the individual's age for his first conversion experience, for it appears from work by Olt (1956) that subjects may have more than one conversion. Some of his subjects reported up to six such experiences while about 30 per cent reported two. Despite this cautionary note, religious conversion, it appears, does not always occur during adolescence; nor apparently is a revivalistic meeting always necessary. Ceaserman (1957) reports the religious conversion of two sex offenders during psychotherapy. Both were midldle-aged males undergoing psychotherapy as a consequence of a sexual offence.

There have been only a limited number of studies which have investigated personality and conversion experience. Christensen (1963) examined twenty-two individuals who had experienced religious conversion and who were undergoing psychoanalytically orientated psychotherapy for incapacitating mental disorders. He identifies what are the predisposing factors leading to the conversion experience and finds they are similar to those described by Carlson (1961) for the acute confusional state. The only distinction in the religious situation is that religious belief is the main precipitating factor and also the main factor in the resolution of the confusion. Carlson concludes that the religious conversion experience seems to be a special instance of the acute confusional state. The basic problem with this work is the character of the sample, not every religious convert ends up with incapacitating mental disorders.

In contrast to Christensen, Allison (1967) explored the personality of twenty Divinity students, using the Rorschach Ink Blot Test. He found that those subjects with sudden conversions had greater amounts of primitive non-logical thought manifestations but were better able to integrate such ideas. They showed greater capacity for regressive experiences of an adaptive kind. Such capacity has been linked in the past with greater tolerance of ambiguity, better imaginative productiveness and less dogmatism. He concludes that his findings do not fit the picture normally used to describe the sudden conversion experience as a pathological, destructive experience resembling psychosis.

Scobie (1967, 1973), using 170 prospective ordinands, found that there were three broad avenues to the religious life, which he named sudden, gradual, and unconscious conversion. The subjects completed six questionnaires : three attempting to measure religious conservatism; Eysenck's Social Attitude Inventory; the Authoritarian 'F' scale; and the shorter version of the Minnesota Multiphasic Personality Inventory. He found that sudden converts were significantly more authoritarian, more conservative in religion and politics and showed less personality control (as defined by Cuadra 1953) and intellectual efficiency than the other conversion types (significance levels beyond P = .05). Sixty-three individuals who claimed that a religious salvation experience (conversion) had changed their lives were investigated by Wilson (1972). He found that they were happier in their affective life and that their perception of the world had changed.

Conversion is a phenomenon occurring quite frequently in the experience of religious people. But it is not apparently a prerequisite for the religious life. Studies of religious people have indicated that many have had no such conversion experience, while others have had more than one. Furthermore the conversion experience is not confined to religious behaviour. Reorientations of a similar nature take place in most areas of human activity. The relevance of the conversion experience to the character of religious beliefs, and the personality factors which may be associated with it, are two important considerations in the psychology of religion. It is for this reason that a detailed examination of the phenomenon of conversion is necessary.

THE MEANING OF CONVERSION

The root meaning of the word is a turning about, or complete and thorough transformation. Unfortunately the word is used very loosely to include the sudden religious illumination, with its attendant high emotional overtones, the slow religious growth or development, and all the varieties or degrees between these two. Because of this it is necessary to qualify the meaning of the word in order to be more explicit. The problem is complicated because the meaning and significance of conversion is not the same for all religious groups. For example, some Protestant sects stipulate a conversion experience in order to qualify for membership of their group, while other religious people view conversion with extreme suspicion, distrusting its emotional character. It would seem that in cases where conversion has unpleasant connotations, the experience itself may still have occurred but is described in some other way (Scobie 1967). If investigators only ask for details of conversion experiences, it may mean that the frequency of the experiences disclosed are reduced by the reluctance of the individuals to accept the terminology used. Therefore, on some occasions, the differences in religious behaviour between groups may be an artifact of terminology rather than of religious experience.

In the following pages the discussion of conversion will be generally restricted to experiences within the Christian religion. This is mainly due to the lack of comparable evidence from other religions.

TYPES OF CONVERSION EXPERIENCE

Individuals acquire their religious beliefs in quite different ways. The pathway to religious faith may be tortuous and contain a series of approaches to, and withdrawals from, any kind of commitment. It is no doubt the case that each conversion is unique and significantly different from every other similar experience. Despite the validity of the claim for individuality, there seem to be three broad avenues or ways by which people become religious. The first method has been variously defined. James (1902) referred to it as the religion of the healthy minded, the once-born variety. Brandon (1960) and Scobie (1967) have described the process as unconscious conversion. The individual in this case is normally brought up in a Christian home, or under the direct influence of Christian people, and whenever he is presented with some aspect of the Christian faith he accepts it. As a consequence he cannot think of a time in his life when he was not a Christian – when he did not accept Christian beliefs. A fairly large number of people seem to gain their religious beliefs in this way. Scobie (1967) found that 30 per cent of his sample of 170 theological students claimed to have followed this pathway to religious belief.

It has already been indicated earlier in the chapter that the process which has attracted most interest from research workers is the sudden conversion experience. The interest aroused by the phenomenon may have created the impression that most religious people have this experience. This is not the case; in Scobie's theological student sample only 20 per cent claimed a sudden conversion experience. This type of conversion is normally described as a crisis experience taking place at a specific moment. The moment may hold special significance for the individual throughout his life, so much so that he is able to give the time and date of the experience years after its occurrence. This point represents the beginning of his Christian life, and he probably regards himself, before the conversion experience, as being a non-Christain. There is a general tendency for the experience to be highly emotional but this is not always the case, and some sudden conversions are particularly lacking in high emotional tone.

By far the most common experience has been called gradual conversion (50 per cent of Scobie's group report the experience). The process or growth of belief extends over a period of time, days, months, or even years. During this period the person moves from a position where he is rejecting Christianity as a whole, or some specific part of it, to a point where this rejection has changed to acceptance. There may be a climax to the process similar to the sudden conversion experience, but any such climax is secondary to the process itself. The process is of prime importance and represents a means whereby the most complicated series of objections to Christian faith can be resolved and commitment accepted.

It is appropriate at this point to consider a number of other aspects of conversion, the average age of converts; how permanent the effects are and what contribution it makes to the general development of belief.

AGE OF CONVERSION

Most of the studies which have examined the age of conversion have found that the majority take place during adolescence. Argyle (1958), reviewing the research dealing with the age of conversion, found that experiences mostly occur between the tenth and twentieth year. The most frequent year in which conversions take place seems to vary with the investigator and perhaps with the date of their research. Fifteen years was the most frequent age of the converts at Billy Graham's British campaign in 1954.

Conversions seems to be predominantly an adolescent phenomenon and those investigators who have emphasised the sexual nature of religion have attempted to link conversion with puberty. The evidence is by no means conclusive. Sexual activity could be an important factor in many conversions but there remains a large proportion of the group whose conversion experience occurs outside the range in which most of the physical changes of puberty take place. Thirty per cent of Starbuck's (1899) subjects reported that their conversion occurred before the onset of puberty, while 47 per cent of Scobie's theological students said their conversion occurred after their seventeeenth birthday. In order to maintain the link with puberty and thus sexual conflict or frustration as the sole explanation of conversion, we need to postulate extreme age variations in the onset of puberty and a near perfect positive correlation between the age of puberty and the age of conversion.

Even then we have no explanation for the small number of individuals who claim to have been converted in their forties.

An important observation made by Argyle is the apparently contradictory finding from investigations of the age of conversion and information about the general religious attitudes of the population. The conversion research indicates that religious interest is at a peak around fifteen to sixteen years of age, while general information indicates a decline in church attendance and an increase in doubt at the same age. Argyle suggests that this is the age when many decisions are made including the one for or against religious commitment. Because only a relatively small number of young people become religious, the conversion phenomenon is concealed by the general decline in religious activity by the vast majority of the younger generation.

THE PERMANENCE OF CONVERSION

The permanence of conversion is another subject that should be briefly considered. In general a conversion is more likely to be permanent if it is gradual (Starbuck 1899). This can be easily understood when a comparison is made between the religious development of the sudden and gradual convert. In gradual conversion the adoption of beliefs is much slower and therefore likely to be more thorough, whereas, the sudden converts' background of religious thought and consideration is somewhat limited. In some cases he may know little more than what he has just heard from the evangelist. It is, therefore, very likely that when he reconsiders his decision he will have doubts about the truth of the arguments used and the value of his religious commitment. He is more likely in retrospect to see the flaws and inadequacies in the evangelist's address and conclude that his response was the result of a hasty and rash decision. The possible change of mind is widely recognised by evangelistic teams who endeavour to minimise the effect by an organised follow-up of new converts.

Despite the systematic counselling plans used by the Billy Graham team, statistics indicate that a year later only about half of the original converts were still attending church (Highet 1957). Although this is a great improvement on earlier revivals it is still an extremely high fall-off rate, but there may be mitigating circumstances. One of the major problems for the counsellor is finding a suitable church for the new convert. If this proves impossible, or the church is too far from his home then the necessary social support is not available, and the possibility of apostasy is increased. The use of church attendance as a measure of religious belief also has its limitations and may be over-estimating the loss of sudden converts. Even when these factors are considered it does seem that gradual converts are more likely to remain church members. However, those sudden converts who do manage to retain their beliefs over the first few months or years do become very staunch supporters of the faith. There are a number of sudden converts from the Billy Graham Campaign who are now clergymen in churches of various denominations. It is also worth noting that 20 per cent of the theological students examined by Scobie were sudden converts now undergoing training for fuller commitment to their faith. It would appear that the distinction between sudden and gradual converts in terms of the permanence of their conversion is greatest at the point of conversion and rapidly diminishes as the time from conversion increases.

THE DEVELOPMENT OF BELIEFS

This examination of beliefs can be divided into pre- and post-conversion development. Of course, for the unconscious conversion group there is no such distinction; it is one continuous process of development. This in itself implies different developmental processes for the conversion types. These processes have already been discussed at the beginning of this chapter in reference to the three conversion types.

Any consideration of development must, of course, start with the religious beliefs of the child. The child's ideas and approach to religion are generally authoritarian in the sense that they are derived from other people, especially parents, a fact substantiated by the empirical study of MacLean (1930). He also found that the child's ideas are unreflective, ideas and concepts are believed despite what would be obvious contradictions to the adult. He found that 73 per cent of a certain group of children agreed that 'God had hands and feet just like a man', while 55 per cent of the same group also agreed with the suggestion that 'God was not like a person at all. He is something like electricity – just an energy that works, keeping things going and making them grow'. There are exceptions, of course, but in general the child's concept of God is not closely bound by logic.

The child's religion is also egocentric. His prayers are filled with personal requests for his own protection and satisfaction, it is only at a later age that altruistic prayers become a significant part of the child's prayer time (Goldman 1964). The concept of God for the child is also crudely anthropomorphic, and also what Clark (1958) describes as superanthropomorphic, or simple human characteristics greatly enlarged such as 'God can see right through the roof' (MacLean 1930). This type of idea in the child is characterised by literalness and concreteness, which puts it in sharp contrast to similar ideas of the mature adult, who normally recognises an inadequacy of language in describing the attributes of God.

The religion of the young child contains many items which have been acquired by rote learning, such as the Lord's Prayer. Thus it becomes obvious that much of the child's religious life is built up through imitation of parents and other adults, but despite this it is also characterised by a certain degree of spontaneity probably provided by his colourful fantasy life.

Harms (1944) found that religious development was characterised by three stages, each occurring at about the age at which significant changes in general thinking are taking place. The first stage is an egocentric period in which religious ideas and concepts are interpreted in terms of the child's own limited experience. For such a child God may be a giant father-like figure living in a world of make-believe common to the fairy stories which he hears. The next stage is one in which religious ideas and concepts are expressed in concrete forms : God has a physical form and characteristics. The final stage is one in which religion becomes personal, and where religious concepts are given spiritual as opposed to physical significance. These are spiritual 'realities' which are beyond or outside material expression.

Goldman (1964) confirms the tripartite development of religious belief, but links it much more closely to developmental stages of logical thinking proposed by Piaget. He names the three stages as (1) intuitive religious thinking, (2) concrete religious thinking and (3) abstract religious thinking. The child passes through each stage and by the time he reaches adolescence his religious thinking has normally reached the abstract level.

It is at this point in the development that the individual begins to challenge the beliefs derived from parents or church and to question their personal relevance and truth. This too is the stage when the different conversion processes may begin to develop. For the unconscious conversion group the process continues with positive or passive acceptance; while for the sudden or gradual convert the process is interrupted and finally given new significance by the conversion experience. For the majority of people (if Argyle's assessment is correct) the process continues in a negative direction, each person, except those in the unconscious conversion group, rejecting religious or Christian beliefs as a personal force at some point in their lives. Many of these people will be recalled to the 'fold' through the sudden or gradual conversion mechanism. The development system so far described is culturally dependent. In cultures other than those with a basic Christian background there may be a different developmental pattern.

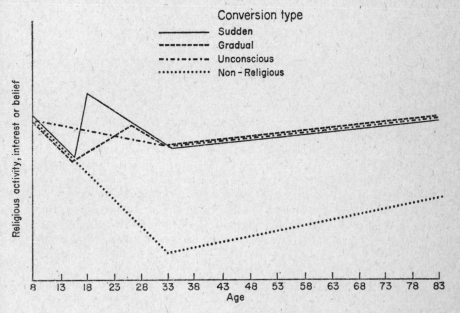

Figure 1. Changes in religious activity with age.

In general the picture is of a gradual decline in religious interest from the child to the young adult. The decline is not apparently the case for the unconscious conversion group and the decline is reversed for gradual and sudden converts. From eighteen to thirty years of age there also appears to be a general decline in religious activity. Most of the information available is concerned with religious behaviour and not religious belief or interest. It has been suggested that the decline in religious observance is a consequence of family and work commitments which may prevent regular attendance at church during this period of life. There is, however, some evidence of a decline in belief in the after-life up to the age of thirty. The practical difficulties cannot account for this decline in belief (Gorer 1955).

From the low point at thirty there is a general increase in religious activity and belief as people get older. This increase in activity seems to be a direct result of age and is not related to historical events common to people of a particular age group. The increase may be a function of both the greater leisure time available and the approaching threat of death and possible illness in old age.

The picture obtained of development is of a decline in religious belief and interest from eight to thirty, while from that point on there is a gradual increase in religious belief and activity. The decline in belief of the unconscious conversion group, if it exists, is much less than the rest of the population, but there is probably a decrease in activity between eighteen and thirty even in this group, with a general increase as the person approaches old age. The sudden and gradual conversion groups show a similar decline in religious belief and behaviour as the non-religious group until adolescence, when there is a sharp increase in faith for sudden converts, and a more gradual increase for gradual converts. The general pattern is then followed, a decline up to the age of thirty and then an overall general increase in religion before old age. Some attempt is made in Figure 1 to represent these differences diagramatically, no statistical accuracy being implied.

The first two variables considered do not seem to have any close relationship with conversion type. There is very little available evidence indicating that conversion plays a significant part in any religion except Christianity. It is likely that conversion experiences do occur in most religions but they do not appear to have the same importance, and mass evangelism is not practised to the same extent. This is an area where future research should give us a far clearer picture of the significance of conversion in non-Christian religions.

In terms of Christian denominations, it is the more fundamentalist groups who emphasis most strongly the need for conversion and who spend a considerable amount of their time trying to effect a conversion experience in others.

SUMMARY

In this chapter three basic classifications of religion have been examined. The classifications of the world religions was the first to be considered. Denomination was the next area discussed. There have been quite a large number of studies in this area especially in the sociological field. The largest proportion of the chapter was devoted to the third classification, religious conversion. Many aspects of conversion were considered, including its relevance to the general development of religious beliefs.

5

Variables of Religious Belief and Behaviour

Part II: Dimensions

The accumulating research evidence soon indicated the complex nature of religious behaviour and it became apparent that more sophisticated statistical tools were required for its exploitation. The technique that many investigators turned to was factor analysis. It is possible by this method to identify factors which are responsible for the variance found in a series of variables. It is essentially an extension of the correlation system. The factors produced can either be independent of one another (orthogonal) or correlated (oblique) but when taken together they account for the amount and pattern of inter-correlations found between all the variables considered. The basic problem for factor analysis is identifying the statistical factors and associating them with actual human characteristics. The technique, as the next few pages will indicate, has provided valuable information about the character of religious behaviour.

Many of the factor analytic studies have used general samples rather than groups of individuals of a specifically religious nature, and usually the investigations were concerned with many different attitudes and not just with religious belief. For example, a study of this kind was conducted by Ferguson (1944) using Thurstone (1931) Attitude Scales. The scale questionnaire contained miscellaneous items on politics, religion, war, etc. He isolated three factors, which he called 'humanitarianism' (relating to attitudes towards capital punishment, treatment of criminals, and war), 'religionism' (relating to orthodox or conservative religious views; measuring attitude to God, evolution and birth control), and 'nationalism' (measuring attitudes to patriotism, Communism, law and censorship).

Eysenck (1944) criticised the previous work done on attitudes by factor analytic methods (including that of Ferguson) mainly on methodological grounds, and maintained that the method he used was a better one. Attitude scores of about 1,500 subjects were factor analysed and two factors identified. The structuring of attitudes he suggests involves two orthogonal axes relating to these two factors : the radical-conservative axis and an axis which he initially referred to as practical/theoretical but subsequently changed in 1953 to tough/tender-mindedness. The religious items tend to come in the conservative/tender-minded quadrant of this dichotomy.

Another study using the general population was undertaken by Cline and Richards (1965) who collected information from a random sample of adults living in Salt Lake City. They used a projective test, an interview, and a questionnaire; the responses were then factor analysed for males and females separately. They isolated twelve factors for females and fourteen for males. There were a number of sex differences : one in particular suggests that for women religious belief and behaviour are directly related but that for men this is not the case. A man is able, it appears, to be extremely active in religious observance and practice, while having doubts and a general fuzziness about his beliefs; or he may be certain and fully committed to his religion in terms of his belief, but not be very active. It is important to note that religious attitudes again appear as an important single factor.

Much research work has been done in an effort to link religious attitudes with personality factors. An interesting experiment in this area using factor analytical techniques calls in question many of the previous findings. Brown (1962), using a modified version of the test used by Thouless (1935) for assessing the strength of religious belief, examined a sample of Adelaide university students. By factor analysis of the replies he was able to isolate two main factors. The first was a religious belief factor having loadings on all the Religious Belief Scales and on Institutionalisation, Denomination, and Authoritarianism. The second factor was a personality factor of neuroticism and anxiety being related to general opinion strength and factual certainty. The important point about this work is that he found that the religious belief factor was independent of the personality measures. Brown concludes that the strength of religious belief is related to acceptance, and membership of the church; whereas matters of opinion and fact on general topics are associated with personality variables, particularly anxiety. This result calls in question much previous work attempting to establish the relationship between religious beliefs and personality characteristics. Brown (1966) extended his investigation, using personality tests and questionnaires purporting to measure twenty-four variables. He isolated eight factors and his results again indicate that religious belief is independent of personality and a ' predominantly cognitive activity, acquired and sustained by social influences and expressed in a number of ways including religious practices '. The work of Fischer and Holl (1968) seems to confirm Brown's finding. They factor analysed the results of questionnaires on religious belief and personality, using Austrian soldiers (most were Roman Catholics) as their subjects. They were able to isolate nine factors and the religiosity factor was virtually independent of personality characteristics except for a correlation with conservatism.

Another group of research workers investigated religion from a different point of view. Instead of examining the general population and looking for evidence of religious belief, they studied specific religious groups in detail. For example, Broen (1957) used individuals selected from two Protestant sects. As a consequence of his own factor analytic investigations of religious attitudes he suggested that it was a mistake to consider religious belief as an uni-dimensional factor and then compare general religiosity with other personality characteristics. He claims that religious belief is multi-dimensional and succeeded in isolating two factors. The first he referred to as ' nearness to God ', a unipolar factor representing and emphasising God as real, accessible, loving and continually present and stressing a ' walking and talking ' relationship with Him. The other, a bipolar factor, he named fundamentalism/ humanitarianism and thought of as a continuum between viewing God as a punishing master, with man as essentially sinful, and seeing man as potentially good and needing little outside support from a deity. The assertion that religious attitudes are multi-dimensional is an important one because it could explain much of the conflicting information collected from various experimental studies.

Allen and Hites (1961) followed the lead of Broen and asked 100 adolescents to complete questionnaires dealing with a number of different religious beliefs and attitudes. They then factor analysed their results and isolated twelve factors, nine of which they identified. ' Man's relation to the Deity ', ' traditional mores of the Church ', ' scepticism ', and ' striving for security ' were the names of some of the factors they discovered. These results add additional evidence to the multi-dimensional character of religious belief.

A novel approach to the problem of religious belief was made by Webb (1965). He gathered information from theological students and then tried to determine if six hypothesised needs could be identified. His analysis isolated eleven needs, some of which he was able to name. These were peace, reverence, curiosity, love, self-abnegation, prayer and meditation, mysticism and people. It would seem that the list has merely indicated that the students are motivated by values having positive loadings within their religious denominations.

The multi-dimensional character of religious belief was again confirmed by King (1967). A group of local Methodists formed his sample and he was able to isolate sixteen factors and twelve clusters from the answers they provided. He concluded that the uni-dimensional view of religious belief should be rejected and suggested that nine of his dimensions required further study.

If religious belief is multi-dimensional what are the types of religious belief that cluster together? Maranell (1968) sent out questionnaires to clergymen of eleven denominations. The questionnaires aimed at measuring eight different aspects of religious belief : fundamentalism, altruism, mysticism, superstition, theism, church orientation, ritualism and idealism. The results after factor analysis produced two factors : the first a conservative/fundamentalist attitude cluster having high loadings on fundamentalism, theism, and superstition; the other a more liberal, socially orientated set of attitudes having high loadings on altruism, idealism, church orientation, and mysticism.

IS RELIGION MULTI-DIMENSIONAL OR UNI-DIMENSIONAL?

The information discussed in the previous paragraphs indicates how useful factor analysis has proved to be. But it is worth making some comment on the controversy between those who support the view that religion is a uni-dimensional phenomenon and those who maintain its multi-dimensional character. Dittes (1969), who examined the evidence from both sides, concludes that theoretical considerations seem to favour a multi-dimensional solution but that much empirical evidence seems to support the uni-dimensional character of religion. Dittes suggests that both approaches are valid. Where broad comparisons are being made within a general population the uni-dimensional features of religion seem most applicable in distinguishing the religious from the non-religious in the selected samples. He also maintains that a deeper analytical investigation of the subject is necessary; in such circumstances the large number of dimensions which play a part in religion would become more significant. This seems a reasonable approach to the problem and encourages the continuance of both types of investigation.

Dittes' explanation of the uni-dimensional/multi-dimensional controversy is given some support by Wearing and Brown (1972). They obtained a single religious factor when using a population having a wide variation in religious commitment. A large number of religious items were used in the questionnaire so the explanation that uni-dimensionality is an artifact of the type and number of religious questions is not confirmed. The nature of the sample seems to be the significant element. Tapp (1971) also found evidence supporting this explanation. He gave a questionnaire to over 12,000 Unitarian Universalists and obtained five factors representing religious behaviour from his analysis. However, an inspection of the loadings on these factors indicated that the first factor was the dominant one and of far greater significance than any of the others. Tapp concluded that, at least for Unitarians, religiosity was less multi-dimensional than for a more traditional religious population such as the Methodist subjects used by King (1967).

It would appear therefore that with more heterogeneous samples having wide-ranging differences in religious commitment a single religious factor will be found. When more homogeneous religious populations are used a greater number of factors seem to emerge. For example King and Hunt (1972) found ten factors were important as aspects of religious behaviour. Multi-dimensionality, at least, for homogeneous religious groups is an important finding. For this reason the rest of the chapter deals with the various dimensions of religious belief and behaviour.

DIMENSIONS

The term dimension usually implies a continuum of change from one end of a scale to the other. There are normally two basic kinds of dimension, unipolar and bipolar. The former refers to a scale variation from the absence of a given quality to its maximum presence, and the latter deals with scale variation from possession of one characteristic to possession of another. The individual can possess both traits in some measure, or only one at the extremes of the range; in other words an inverse relationship holds for the two variables. For example, political attitudes can be measured and bipolar dimensions produced varying from the radical to the conservative pole; the more radical the political beliefs the less conservative the score and vice versa. If one is concerned with measuring political interest then a unipolar scale could be devised ranging from those who are very interested to those who are uninterested in politics, that is from presence to absence of a given characteristic. Eysenck's Neuroticism Scale is unipolar; subject's responses range from very high emotionality to very low emotionality. On the other hand his scales for Radicalism/Conservatism, Tough/Tender-mindedness, Introversion/Extraversion are all bipolar scales. The lower the measure on one variable, the higher the measure on the other (see Figure 2, p. 65).

If the claim that religious belief is multi-dimensional is justified it means that it is a mistake to try and assess it on one variable; for example a unipolar scale from belief to unbelief, or a bipolar scale from pro-religious attitudes to anti-religious attitudes, unless one is making broad comparisons within the general population of a country or using a heterogeneous sample. Therefore, a number of dimensions are usually required to provide an adequte measure of the individual's religious attitudes and activity. The same claim is made by Eysenck for political attitudes. He maintains that not only is the radical/conservative dimension necessary, but also another dimension which he calls tough/tender-mindedness. In other words, he claims that political attitudes are two factored or bi-dimensional. There is no need to stop at two dimensions; in theory there can be any number. The number of dimensions suggested for religious belief seems to depend on the experimental evidence considered. Broen (1957) refers to two dimensions; King (1967) claims that nine of his dimensions needed further examination, and Maranell (1968) lists eight dimensions which formed two clusters or factors. Perhaps there is a certain amount of confusion between factor and dimension. Briefly, if a number of dimensions cluster together they may form a single factor, and it is then possible for a researcher to devise a single scale for measuring that factor. The basic assumption underlying the process is that the factor is the cause, or directly related to the cause, of the variation found within the dimensions. So, by attempting to measure the factor directly the investigator is gaining the same information he would collect by the indirect means of using a number of dimensions. This method seems to be logically sound and in practice very desirable. Unfortunately, there is a certain arbitrariness about the selection of the number of factors. It depends on the statistical procedure adopted and on the degree of error variance the experimenter regards as reasonable. Some researchers look for further factors, while others would refer to error variance. An additional problem has already been mentioned, namely that the number of identifiable factors tend to vary with the range of data analysed. In consequence the number of factors listed shows as much variation as the list of possible dimensions. Broen (1957)

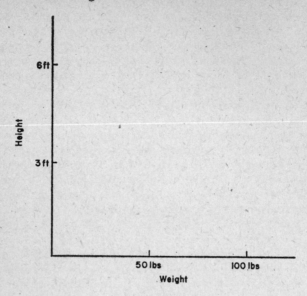

Two unipolar dimensions

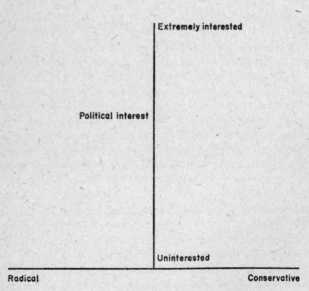

One unipolar , one biopolar dimensions

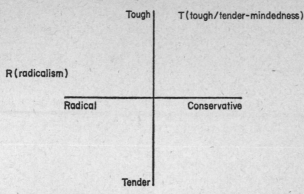

Figure 2. Unipolar and bipolar dimensions (Eysenck's R and T scales)

provides two factors while King (1967) claims to have isolated sixteen.

CLASSIFYING RELIGIOUS VARIABLES

One useful method of classifying the numerous religious variables is offered by Glock (see Glock and Stark 1965). They suggest five groups or dimensions, three of which correspond very closely to the three broad areas of religious behaviour described in chapter 1. The five dimensions are referred to as :

(1) religious beliefs (ideological dimension)
(2) religious practices (ritualistic dimension)
(3) religious feeling (experimental dimension)
(4) religious knowledge (intellectual dimension)
(5) religious effects (consequential dimension)

These last two categories need some comment, they seem to be less clearly differentiated than the first three. Any measure of religious knowledge will of course be affected by the intelligence of the subjects used. If intelligence is held constant, measures of religious information may be simply indicating religious interest or commitment and probably falling within the scope of the experimental dimension. Another basic problem is the extent of religious knowledge tested. Many devoted religious people will have a detailed but limited range of religious information concerned principally with their own faith, while an atheist may have a much broader range of information, though at a superficial level.

Some allowance must be made for ranges in religious information, otherwise results may be misleading.

C

The consequential dimension deals with the effects of religion on practical conduct, and is a measure of the influence that the individual's religious faith has on his daily life. In includes the immediate effects of religion such as peace of mind or burdens lifted, etc., and the promise of future rewards such as salvation and immorality. It would be valuable to examine several areas where beliefs do seem to have a significant influence on a person's behaviour.

Moral behaviour

It is argued that the beliefs of the religious person must affect his code of conduct. The Christian religion provides its own ethical system, and to be a Christian necessitates conformity to this code. This is a code of 'love', love God and love your neighbour as yourself. The outworkings of this code in practical behaviour are a little more difficult to formulate. In general the Christian Church has indicated that the Ten Commandments are a brief outline of the practical behaviour associated with the code of love. But recently this has been challenged by certain of the more liberal sectors of Protestantism who think that general rules can mean a violation of the law of love. In this way two different dimensions of belief can arise which may affect moral behaviour; one, a measure of how vital the Christian religion is to an individual, and thus how essential it is to observe the ethical code, and two, a measure of the deviation from the strict interpretation of the code of love as observance of the Ten Commandments. This second dimension would be very closely associated with conservatism/liberalism in theology or religion. If it is assumed that more vital beliefs are held more intensely, the first dimension would have a high correlation with intensity of religious belief. It is probable that the intense conservatives would act in strict obedience to the Ten Commandments and that the intense liberals would order their lives by their own interpretation of the code of love. Those whose religion is not intense may be 'conventionally religious', the conservatives upholding the status quo, and the liberals following a more laissez faire system of religious belief. As a consequence the more 'intense' Christians may have a greater concern for the welfare of others, and may play a more active part in those social reforms which try to help people in distress. Perhaps the intense liberals would be more prevalent in such participation for they are less tied to the existing religious structure.

Imitation of Christ or discipleship

Both these terms imply a similar practice – the attempt made by individuals to imitate Christ in all the various circumstances of their life. In other words they act out the consequences of their beliefs, i.e. consequential dimension. Thus, when faced with a particular situation, before acting or making any kind of decision they try and determine what Christ would do in a similar position, and then try to act accordingly.

The imitation of Christ, or discipleship, involves trying to do what Christ would do, and not making decisions on the basis of self-interest. The central problem is deciding what action Christ would have taken in a given siuation. It is obviously based on the individual's preconceived ideas of the character of Christ, but as these in the main are based on the Biblical narrative, the exercise does have some objectivity. Problems only arise in situations where there is no Biblical parallel, or where there are conflicting Biblical illustrations to the life situation. The exercise then takes on the similitude of living up to the individual's own standards. In practice, however, this manner of life does lead to a greater piety and love for one's neighbour, and thus does reflect the generally accepted character of Christ. It would be interesting to know just what effect the hidden maxim in the exercise, ' Think before you act' has on subsequent behaviour.

Immortality and the Second Advent

The belief in immortality and the Second Coming of Christ does have a tremendous effect on behaviour. Many of the more extreme Protestant sects have often predicted the date of the Second Coming of Christ, and have been so convinced that they have waited patiently on mountain tops for their Lord to appear. Far from being discouraged when the appearance did not take place they have gone back to their churches, made another prediction, and been even more active in the propagation of their beliefs.

The Christian concept of immortality has probably played a large part in enabling martyrs to bear the tremendous amount of pain involved in being burnt alive, in some cases without even a murmur. Whatever the actual physical explanation may be, undoubtedly the thought of immortality, ' to be with Christ, which is far better' was compensation enough for any pain the fire produced.

These are extreme cases of the use to which belief in the Second Coming and immortality are put, but how far do these beliefs affect the average Christian? It is necessary to examine the Christian concept of immortality before an estimate of its effects can be given. The orthodox doctrine of immortality teaches that there is immortality for all, but for believers it (Heaven) is to be desired as infinitely better than the greatest joys of this life, while for those who do not believe it (Hell) means greater anguish than that ever experienced on this earth. For the believer immortality is to be with Christ. Thus for the Christian it implies that he is in this life like ' a stranger and pilgrim in a foreign land '. This means that ideally the Christian is disinterested in the materialistic concerns which are the diet of his contemporaries. Thus monks and nuns are able to deny themselves all the material comforts and luxuries of the world for the greater prize which is to come.

The orthodox concept of the Second Advent is that Christ will come to this world again, not this time as a ' baby and Saviour, but as King and Judge '. He will come when He is least expected, ' in the twinkling of an eye or as a thief in the night ' and believers should be ready prepared to be ' caught up to meet Him '. Thus they must live with one eye to the future and since they do not know when He will come, they are commanded to be ready which gives added impetus to the business of living a morally upright life and makes spiritual values seem even more important.

Evangelism and Proselytism

There are certain sectors of the Christian church which are termed ' Evangelical ', that is they believe that the Christian gospel must be actively brought to the attention of non-believers. It is something more than an attempt to increase the size and influence of their own denomination, but is an attempt to get people to believe in, and live for, Christ, rather than an effort to make people conform to the discipline and dogma of a particular denomination. There are of course cases where conformity is demanded, but the devout ' evangelical ' believes it is his duty to preach Christ with the minimum of denominational strings. His main object is to persuade people to commit their lives to Christ; the content of the belief is a subsequent and secondary factor, Billy Graham for example.

Personal evangelism is the name given to private talks the evangelical may have with his friends or acquaintances about Christ. The zealous evangelical looks for opportunities in his individual conversations with people to talk about Christ or religion with this ultimate purpose in mind, the conversion of his listener. (A fuller discussion of conversion will be found in chapter 4).

Public evangelism has the same object, but it is an organised method of putting the claims of Christ to the general public. It ranges from small 'open air meetings' (where an evangelist speaking in a public place tries to arouse the interest of passersby) to the large public meetings of the Billy Graham variety. Many of the small denominations and sects indulge in the former type of public evangelism. Personal evangelism forms an integral part of the public evangelism procedure, in so far that each public meeting (if successful) is followed by personal interviews. Trained 'counsellors' meet any person who has responded to the challenge provided by the speaker, and talks to them individually about the Christian faith. This technique is normally referred to as 'counselling', at least in the larger evangelistic meetings.

Proselytism is the word reserved in Christian circles for the activity of attempting to convert people to one's own denomination. The main emphasis in this type of activity is outward conformity to the denominational pattern, rather than a complete involvement in the Christian gospel. What you do rather than what you are, would be a simple way of distinguishing between proselytism and evangelism. Of course it is possible to combine the two.

The purpose of discussing these last four topics was to indicate the tremendous effect that beliefs can have on an individual's behaviour. It is thus apparent that the consequential dimension is very important. However, the amount of systematic research done in this area and in the intellectual dimension is quite small and often the information that does become available is usually included within the framework of the other dimensions. Therefore, a three group classification system seems the most useful one to use in the present circumstances.

There is also some doubt whether the dimensions are in any sense independent of one another. Faulkner and De Jong (1966) produced the 5–D scale which measures the five dimensions of ritual, experimental, ideological, intellectual and consequential. But work by Clayton (1971) indicated a close correspondence between the scales and he questioned the value of five separate scales.

RELIGIOUS BELIEFS

Perhaps one of the most important dimensions in this area is religious conservatism. There are two aspects of conservatism which

need to be clarified : ' content' conservatism and 'manner' conservatism. Content conservatism is concerned with the type of
beliefs a person holds. Religious people may belong to institutions
with widely differing beliefs, like Hinduism and Islam, and even
Christians do not believe exactly the same thing. Members of the
same denomination also show considerable variety in the beliefs
they hold. It is necessary to adopt a particular base line or
criterion in order to compare individual or group variations in
religious belief. The usual criterion selected is the traditional Biblical
or orthodox belief (or some equivalent standard in another religion)
where the Bible is interpreted literally and fundamentalist principles
are defended. It is then possible to measure the degree of deviation
from this standard. A person or group which agrees with all items
of this kind on a scale, and disagrees with all others, will be extremely conservative. It is, of course, essential in the construction
of such a scale to have test items representative of the whole range
of religious beliefs, conservative, middle and radical. The base line
is really a matter of convenience; it does not make much sense
to talk about absolute conservatism or total conservatism. It is
usual to restrict the use of these scales to comparisons between individuals and groups and between groups. Used in this way one
individual will gain a more conservative score than another, or
one group will be shown as more radical than the next. Such a
procedure avoids the problem of searching for the impossible,
the most conservative attitude to a particular item of faith that an
individual or group could possibly hold. The dimension of religious
conservatism can be viewed as the varying attitudes of individuals
or groups to Biblical orthodoxy or fundamentalism. The Conservatism Scale attempts to measure how radical or conservative the
beliefs are. It is concerned with content.

Another type of conservatism deals with the manner or style
in which beliefs are held and is independent of content. This is
what Rokeach has called dogmatism, a measure of the open and
closed mind. A high score on such a scale indicates a dogmatic and
rigid adherence to a set of beliefs which can be conservative or
radical in content. It was Gilmore (1969) who pointed out that
even those groups with very fundamentalist beliefs vary greatly in
their dogmatism score; indicating that very conservative beliefs
can be held in a non-dogmatic way. For example, an individual
may believe in the inspiration of Scripture but he may still be open
to the possibility that other ideas about the Bible could be equally
valid. Dogmatism is a personality variable and as such it influences
religious belief and behaviour, but it is not a religious dimension.

People can be dogmatic in other areas, such as politics and ethics. Religious conservatism then provides a means of measuring individual or group attitudes to Biblical orthodoxy. An individual's score on the scale may not necessarily match that of the notional mean of the denomination of which he is a member but may be very different. Often there is a considerable range of scores gained by individuals belonging to the same denomination. However, some denominations like the Plymouth Brethren, seem very homogeneous in belief and their members gain scores within an extremely narrow range. In order to be accepted members may have to conform closely to group norms, and, for example, uphold the Biblical teaching on the virgin birth. In contrast members of the Church of England with its collection of distinctive groups from Anglo-Catholic to Evangelical or Low Church would have a very wide range of scores. The other main Protestant denominations would also present a similar variation, but probably not as extensive as that of the Church of England.

There have been attempts to place the denominational groups along the religious conservatism dimension; and provided one is willing to ignore the overlap of scores this may be a useful procedure. In recent years there seems to have been a shrinking of denominational barriers and a very significant increase in the range of scores on religious conservatism (these two facts are obviously related). The extent of the overlap between denominations is now so great that it is more useful to concentrate on religious conservatism as a measure of religious belief, rather than denominational allegiance. A more acceptable alternative to denominational allegiance is theological training. It has been found that within the Church of England an examination of the attitudes expressed by the theological colleges gives a good indication of the religious beliefs of the clergy trained there. It is possible that the finding can be applied to all denominations, and probably represents the interaction of selection and training. Students may modify their beliefs according to the instruction they receive, but there is also a tendency for prospective ministers to attend a college which propounds a theological attitude similar to their own.

Very closely associated with religious conservatism is 'theological position'. By this is meant the name or label a person gives to his particular system of religious beliefs, Catholic, Evangelical, Protestant, etc. It is often more than just an individual's attitude, for it also identifies the person with a particular reference group. To a large extent theological position has taken the place of denominational grouping, and in many respects they are more appropriate; for with the increasing range of beliefs held within denominations, these terms have served to group together individuals of like mind. Although these terms do not have the same status as the denominational ones, they frequently are affiliated to organisations through which they are able to express themselves. For example, the Inter-Varsity Fellowship expounds the opinions and attitudes of the Conservative Evangelical. Presumably individuals gain social support and reinforcements for their beliefs when they claim membership of a like-minded group. Not all Christians want to claim a theological position, and a few, especially at the radical end of the religious conservatism scale refuse to use them. There are also large numbers of Christians who are unable to claim a theological position because they lack the necessary theological sophistication.

However, the groups are not as precise as the previous paragraph may have indicated. For while on certain basic issues there is a consensus of belief; on peripheral issues there may be a variety of opinion. For example, the Conservative Evangelical accepts a fundamentalist position in terms of doctrine, but preferences in ritual do vary and denominational allegiances are thus retained.

Another bipolar dimension proposed by Broen (1957) is named fundamentalism/humanitarianism. This is basically a measure of the individual's attitude to man. And the fundamentalist end of the scale the concept of God. God is a God of wrath and man is essentially sinful, deserving only punishment from God the Master, while at the other end of the continuum man is seen in a more optimistic light. He is essentially good and capable, able to fulfil his purpose without needing significant support or help from God. This dimension is very closely related to religious conservatism. The fundamentalist concept of God and man is based on the Bible which in general paints a picture of a wrathful God and man as sinful. The humanitarian concept is not representative of Biblical orthodoxy, and would be placed at the radical end of the religious conservatism scale. It seems unnecessary to duplicate scales or dimensions. This particular dimension concentrates on one religious question, i.e. the concept of man's nature, and can be seen as a subscale of religious conservatism, which may include this concept, along with a number of others. It is a valid measure, but may be less reliable because of its concentration on just one issue. In addition, the use of humanitarianism as a label may be a little misleading if all Broen wishes to contrast is the pessimistic with the optimistic view of man, which is the impression given by his definitions.

These variables are not the only means by which religious belief may be examined but they do constitute, especially religious conservatism, a large area where research has provided useful information. One of the most important findings which necessitates further consideration is the relationship between religious conservatism, conversion type, and other factors.

Scobie (1967) found that sudden converts scored significantly higher on religious conservatism than both the gradual and unconscious conversion groups and the gradual conversion group was significantly more conservative than the unconscious conversion group. Some of the variations can be attributed to differences in theological training, but there is evidence that significant differences occur even when theological college training is held constant.

There are two possible explanations for the relationship between conversion experience and religious conservatism. It is claimed that conversion has a Biblical basis. The often quoted words of Christ to Nicodemus, 'You must be born again' (John 3:7, AV) are frequently interpreted as a general directive demanding a conversion experience. St. Paul's conversion on the Road to Damascus is seen as the model conversion experience – a sudden conversion experience. Religious beliefs which are closely tied to Scripture are held by fundamentalists and biblical literalists who come by definition at the extreme conservative end of the religious conservatism scale. This would explain why sudden converts are more conservative than both the gradual and unconscious conversion group.

The same conclusion can be drawn from the fact that it is normally the theologically conservative group within Protestantism which organises evangelistic meetings designed to elicit sudden conversions. The evangelist, the counsellors and those who take part in the follow-up work will therefore, in most cases, be religious conservatives. These people will be the sudden converts main source of religious information and unless this early learning in his religious life proves inadequate it will determine the character of his religious beliefs and he is therefore more likely to be a religious conservative. Many investigators have found personality factors correlating with religious conservatism. For example, Dreger (1952) using the conservatism/liberalism dichotomy produced two groups carefully matched on a number of criteria. He was then able to conclude from using various projective tests (e.g. T.A.T. and Rorschach) that the religious conservatives had a greater need for dependency than the liberals. This finding may tie in with some of the negative characteristics of conservatives found by Stewart and Webster (1970). They devised a Theological Conservatism Scale and administered it to Baptist ministers and deaconesses in New Zealand. The results indicated that those isolated as theologically conservative by using the scale were more inclined to be dogmatic, generally conservative, ethnocentric, rigid, insensitive, rejecting human nature, and not good at inter-personal relationships as indicated by the personality measures used. The theological liberals tended to produce the opposite pattern.

Some attempt too has been made to try to relate physiological factors to religious conservatism. For example, King and Funkenstein (1957) investigated different reactions to stress and found that subjects who responded to stress by anger directed outwards at the experimenter (related to a nor-epinephrine-like cardiovascular reaction to stress) tended to picture their fathers as stern disciplinarians, to have conservative religious beliefs and came from families who attended church regularly. Those subjects who responded to stress by anger directed inwards against themselves or anxiety (epinephrine-like cardiovascular reaction to stress) claimed that their fathers were non-dominant in discipline, had more liberal religious views and came from families where church-going was infrequent.

It is possible that conservatism is a personality variable which determines both political and religious attitudes. If this is the case a significant correlation should be found between religious and political conservatism, which is indeed the case. Scobie (1967) found a highly significant correlation between the two types of conservatism, well beyond the .01 level of confidence. This relationship still holds true even when authoritarianism, a significant correlate of both types of conservatism, is controlled by partial correlation techniques.

Another interesting finding by Scobie is the interrelation between religious conservatism, political conservatism and conversion type. It seems that sudden conversion experience predisposes the the individual to adopt conservative religious views, despite his political attitudes. Gradual and unconscious conversion seems to make the individual more liable to adopt radical religious beliefs, despite a conservative political attitude. The same relationship seems to hold true for voting intention as well as for political attitude.

TABLE 2: CONVERSION TYPE AND VOTING INTENTION

Voting Intention

	Sudden	Gradual	Unconscious	Total
Conservative	21	30	16	67
Liberal	3	20	10	33
Labour	4	29	19	52
Total	28	79	45	152

(X^2 significant .02 level of confidence.)

Table 2 (above) indicates a significant relationship between conversion type and voting intention with sudden converts mainly supporting the conservative party while members of the gradual and unconscious groups tend to support the more radical parties.

One of the main variables influencing political conservatism is social class. Reference has already been made to the influence of social class on voting behaviour. In addition Scobie found a significan correlation between political conservatism and a measure of social status. It indicated that the more radical individuals gained higher scores on social status scales. This is in opposition to the result found for voting behaviour. The same thing seems to apply to religious conservatism; religious radicals have higher scores on social status scales, whereas conservative supporters who are usually upper or middle class appear to be religious conservatives. It is possible that for a religious sample political attitude scales and voting intention are quite separate. An alternative explanation could be that the social status scales are measuring aspiration for higher social status rather than the actual social status. But if the relationship between conversion type and religious and political conservatism is linked to social status, then as a higher proportion of sudden converts support the Conservative party, their class composition should show a higher percentage of upper and middle class and a lower percentage of working class than the other two conversion types.

TABLE 3: CONVERSION TYPE AND CLASS COMPOSITION

	CLASS		
	Upper	Middle	Working
Full group	8%	56%	36%
Sudden Converts	3%	55%	41%
Gradual Converts	8%	51%	41%
Unconscious Converts	12%	64%	24%

(Scobie 1967)

The figures in the table show the exact opposite to the anticipated results. In fact the unconscious conversion group seems to have the highest representation of upper- and middle-class subjects. In other words, this finding supports the finding that religious radicals have higher social status. Why then should sudden converts and religious conservatives be more politically conservative and more likely to support the Conservative party? The answer must be connected with their religious experience and religious beliefs and not related to social class. These findings, therefore, indicate that social class is an important factor in political conservatism, but not in religious conservatism. There is one further possibility, that the social mobility that religious commitment may bring contributes to the greater political conservatism. There is more room for social mobility among the sudden and gradual converts than among the unconscious conversion group since many of the latter group are already at the upper end of the social scale. Therefore, if the development of political conservatism is connected with social mobility or aspiration then we would expect the sudden or gradual converts to be more politically conservative.

It is possible that the conflicting results are due entirely to the way religious belief is measured. Some dimensions may be relatively independent of personality factors, while other dimensions may have significant correlations with these same factors. In order to clarify this problem further research is needed in the area.

As we shall see in chapter 7 the correlation between religious conservatism and authoritarianism, prejudice, ethnocentrism, and dogmatism seems to be well-established. Scobie found this was true even for theological students. It may be that these scales are biased against religious conservatives as much as Rokeach claims the authoritarian scale is biased against political conservatives. If this is true, then in the dogmatism scale he has not succeeded in reducing the bias, for religious conservatism also correlates with dogmatism. It is surprising that sudden converts who seem to be most committed to religious belief and observances should show a prejudice which is expressly forbidden by Christian teaching. It is possible that devotion to the in-group, all Christian believers, produces intolerance of all those outside their group such as Jews. Alternatively, the beliefs which for them are realistic evaluations, such as 'all unbelievers are bound for hell', are scored and interpreted as prejudice and intolerance by the tests. The Bible provides this dichotomy, the emphasis on the brotherhood of man on the one hand, and the threat of punishment and suffering for the unbeliever on the other. The problem is whether the former should be referred to as humanitarianism and the latter as intolerance and prejudice. This area needs further investigation in order to clarify the relationship of religious conservatism to prejudice and authoritarianism.

Most investigations of religious conservatism and intelligence have found a negative correlation. A possible explanation is suggested in chapter 7 that the more intelligent are less conforming and they are, therefore, more likely to be radical in their religious beliefs. Social status may be another important variable that ought to be taken into account. Although Scobie found little evidence of a significant relationship between religious conservatism and intelligence, there was a significant negative correlation between religious conservatism and social status measures. In addition he found a highly significant positive correlation between status and intelligence. It would therefore seem possible that the link between conservatism and intelligence may be due to social status. Scobie's sample was intellectually more homogeneous than the general religious population and so social status may be an even more important variable in groups with a wider range of intelligence scores.

Brown and Lowe (1951) found that a group of Bible Students scored high in the M.M.P.I. hysteria scale. This result might suggest that religious conservatives as a whole (Bible students would normally score high on religious conservatism) would score high in hysteria. In other words, there would be a high correlation between religious conservatism and hysteria and neuroticism in general. Scobie, however, found no significant correlations between religious conservatism and hysteria, or any of the other measures he used for neuroticism. There seems little evidence therefore, of a significant relationship between neuroticism and religious conservatism. The positive results that have occurred may be linked with conversion experience, which might be of the extreme variety in certain Bible student groups, rather than religious conservatism.

There also seems little evidence of a significant relationship between religious conservatism and the extraversion/introversion scale. Scobie did find that religious radicals were just significantly more impulsive (Eysenck claims that impulsivity is one aspect of extraversion) but as Brown's (1962) findings indicate, both neuroticism and extraversion seem to be relatively independent of religious belief. Perhaps these variables play a more important part in conversion experiences.

Another important area of religious belief where there are considerable variations of emphasis is concerned with the individual's attitudes to authority. In chapter 1 (page 8) reference was made to the various attitudes towards authority that can be found in the Church. It can be seen that such attitudes represent a further dimension of religious belief and attitude. At one end of the scale are individuals who expect authoritative directives from their Church and accept and act upon them because they are Church pronouncements. At the opposite end are subjects who do not accept Church authority, but maintain individual autonomy and self-reliance. To some extent the various attitudes are independent of the denominations to which the individual belongs. But there are Churches which demand subjection to authority. In such cases there will be relatively few individuals at the self-reliant end of the scale.

The personality variables of authoritarianism and dogmatism have relevance here. One characteristic of the authoritarian personality is a willingness to submit to authority outside of himself, and Rokeach thinks of the dogmatic individual as one who is willing to accept proof by authority. Further comment will be made on this issue when the dogmatism factor is considered. It should be pointed out that a great deal of religious belief is based on divine authority and so in general religious people may be more dogmatic. The important point to note in the present context is the possibility that high correlations will be found for religious people between authoritarianism or dogmatism, and measures of attitude to authority. It is interesting to note that the only personality attitude variable found by Brown (1962) to correlate significantly with his measures of religious belief was a shortened version of the Authoritarianism Scale.

An individual's attitude to the Church is another important variable and closely allied to attitudes to authority. In a sense the Church represents one source of authority and a person who appreciates the authority of the Church will normally extol its virtues and emphasise its place and significance in society. This variable is probably a bipolar dimension ranging from extremely positive attitudes to the Church and its authority, to an emphasis of the individual's rights to make his own decisions without the pronouncements of the Church. Brown uses the labels institutionalisation and individualism to describe the variable. He, however, uses separate scales to measure them and does not treat them as a single dimension. The description of the poles of the dimension indicates that it is a measure of attitude to authority in reference to the Church as an institution and not so much to Divine Authority, or the authority of church officials.

Other dimensions of religious belief have been suggested. For example McConahay and Hough (1973) have devised a love/ guilt orientative dimension of Christian belief. They associate love and guilt with self and other orientations to give four dimensions. A fifth dimension of conservatism is culture orientated. They found no relationship between this dimension and instrinsic/extrinsic dimensions. But they did find, as might have been expected, that the love-other dimension was negatively related to guilt and unrelated with the love-self scale. We have spent considerable time discussing religious conservatism and the variables associated with it, because many of the investigations within the field of religious behaviour have made extensive use of the dimension. The significant relationship between religious conservatism and conversion type supports the view put forward in this book that religious experiences determine to a large extent religious attitudes and behaviour.

RELIGIOUS PRACTICES

There are many activities which can be allocated to the religious practices dimension. The division by denomination which was discussed earlier in this chapter could also be viewed as an expression of religious practice. But denominational allegiance is not strictly a dimension, it is a classification, and for this reason it was discussed in chapter 4.

A measure of religious behaviour often used is frequency of church attendance. Sometimes a simple classification system is operated, such as non-attenders, infrequent attenders, and regular attenders. Alternatively, some interval measurement may be attempted like the number of times an individual attends church during a month. While this measure is quite a useful indice of religious activity it is subject to certain limitations. People attend church for a number of different reasons, many of which have no religious significance, but will still be reflected in this measure of religious activity. In addition each denomination places a different emphasis on church attendance, so comparison of individuals with different denominational backgrounds may give erroneous results. In order to overcome this limitation it is necessary to look in greater depth at several of the more common religious practices.

Worship and Ritual
One of the central features of most religions and especially Christianity is worship. It is worship which does most to set religions apart from purely ethical systems of belief and conduct.

It is very difficult to understand what are the underlying motives

for worship, but there have been attempts to explain its development in the life of man by using the concepts of fear. This approach
suggests that there are two possible aspects of worship : appease-
ment and control. Primitive man was afraid of what the powers
greater than himself could do, so worship had to be given to appease
their wrath and thus avoid personal injury. Man wanted food and
protection, etc., and so worship was given in order to induce the
powers that surrounded him to provide his needs and wants.
Elaborate rituals were devised with these two ends in mind, to
avoid disaster and punishment, and to control outside events for
the betterment of himself or his community. These 'rituals', by
the law of chance, received 'partial reinforcement' (i.e. a particular activity is reinforced by sporadic rewards. This type of reinforcement has been found to make learning more permanent) and
thus persisted. According to this explanation the whole emphasis of
worship seems to be that of control – controlling the gods to avoid
their wrath and gain their favour, motivated by the fear of
consequences and the inability to control the unknown. Control is
the objective and fear the motive.

When this explanation is applied to religion today it is found
to have equal efficacy. Many religious people still use God as an
explanation of the unknown, and as there is less that scientific man
cannot explain, their God has a progressively smaller domain. The
claim that God gives a purpose to life is a more sophisticated
version of the argument : 'A man cannot see any purpose in
creation, or to his own life without the concept of God'. But of
course if science can provide a good alternative argument or explanation, then God's domain is smaller still. This explanation of worship
poses several problems for religion. It is possible to suggest that
prayer is only an attempt to obtain what we want or need, that
confession and worship are only attempts to avoid punishment and
secure favour, and that thanksgiving and praise are merely attempts
to put 'God' in a good mood towards us. Even when it is claimed
that there is more to worship than this, such as the desire for unity
and fellowship with the Godhead, the mechanisms of fear and control still seem applicable. Perhaps this is one of the weaknesses of the
theory that it seems to explain too much, for it would seem that no
justification of worship could escape from explanation by this dual
mechanism. The counter-explanation of religion offered by its
adherents stresses worship as an expression of love and giving
God His due. It would seem in the last analysis that both are true
to some extent, that man in religion, as in all other walks of life,
is a creature of mixed motives.

The explanation of worship discussed above seems to equate religion to magic, for magic is an undeniable attempt to control supernatural forces. Magic itself is another problem but the similarities to some aspects of Christianity need to be considered. The main similarity is that of ritualisation. Elaborate rituals are devised for black and white magic 'circles' in which the words and actions must be adhered to strictly, and the secrecy of these rituals jealously guarded from outsiders. Part of the whole essence of such movements is the possession of new secrets as the individual progresses in the movement. In like fashion ritualisation in Christian worship does have word-and-action-formulas which must be observed and a decision has to be made by the believer as to whether these are essential to the act itself, or merely an attempt at uniformity of presentation. There would appear to be a variety of opinions about this within Christendom, and it has been suggested already that ritualisation is another denominational variable of the Christian Church. Those who claim that certain rituals are essential for Christian worship will obviously have more difficulty in defending themselves against the accusation that religion is sophisticated magic.

It is impossible to discuss the subject of worship without reference to the behaviour and beliefs associated with the Christian rite of Communion, for most Christians the focal point of all Christian worship.

There are at least three concepts of the main purpose of this act of worship: it is seen as the sacrificial offering of Christ to God in atonement of man and God, as the uniting of the participants into the Godhead via Christ, and as a fellowship meal with Christ and one another in remembrance of His death. Probably each sector of the Christian community would claim all three in some sense of the words, except perhaps for the first which is particularly associated as the 'Catholic' interpretation and alien to a large part of Protestantism. Depending on the theological position one of these concepts will be stressed to the neglect of the others. The religious behaviour varies from treating the 'elements' (bread and wine) as one would treat a king, which is associated with the belief that the bread and wine have in some sense become the Body and Blood of Christ, and thus merit reverence and royal treatment, to treating the elements as almost an optional extra, as indicated by the substitution in some communities of water for wine, the full stress being fellowship in obedience to Christ.

The actual eating of the Body and the Blood, can be interpreted on a purely spiritual plane, with no envisagement of an actual physical change in the elements, otherwise there might be an accusation of cannibalistic practice. Unless the matter is spiritualised the link with ancient religions and their sacrificial systems (the Pauline reference is to meat offered to idols) is obvious. Perhaps this is an example where religious beliefs are so strong as to overcome the acquired aversion of Western society to eating human flesh; if not, it must be postulated either that such believers do not think about the implications of their beliefs, or that they indulge in mental gymnastics to get round the problem. It is of course possible that despite the official formularies of their Churches, the members do not actually believe such doctrines.

The problem of worship and ritual is an area where research is urgently required. It is common knowledge that invidiual Churches differ in the variety and extent of the ritual they prefer at their services, but ritualism is a dimension which has been least used in the psychological study of religious belief and behaviour. Ritual is historically derived and it therefore seems very likely that those who favour ritualistic religion will also support the organisations which try to maintain traditional social and political values, that is they will be more conservative in politics. This argument could be equally applied to religious beliefs and thus there should be a significant relationship between ritualism and religious conservatism, and in consequence religious conventionalism.

Undoubtedly ritualism is an area where research work is urgently needed in the psychology of religion. Relatively little is known about the relationships of this variable and other measures of religious belief, and personality traits. The dimension is a measure of the extent to which people accept, employ, or enjoy ritual within their religious life. In the medieval Church ritual formed a basic part of the religious life of almost every Christian, but with the Reformation a change took place, Roman Catholic and Eastern Orthodox Churches retaining their medieval rituals to a greater extent than the Protestants who developed less elaborate rituals, in some cases the ritual being very simple and in others almost non-existent. The basic problem is to find an acceptable definition of ritual. Usually it is considered as the prescribed order of performing religious services. But almost every religious group (even the Quakers) have their prescribed order. The factor which appears to discriminate between the groups is the relative importance attached to the ritual as an end in itself. The extreme ritualists would claim that unless the order is maintained and observed in strict detail, the whole service loses its efficacy, and is virtually invalid and irrelevant. At the opposite end of the scale the prescribed order is seen only as a convenience and can be drastically modified at any time. The reason for the same order persisting over the years is a function of its attractiveness to the group; the known is preferred to the unknown and the well-established to the novel. It is therefore possible to measure ritualism in terms of the individual's attachment to the prescribed order of his religious group. The Christian denominations can also be placed on a continuum from extreme ritualism to non-ritualism. Beginning at the ritualist end we find the Roman Catholic and Eastern Orthodox Churches followed by the Episcopal Church, the other major Protestant denominations, and finally at the other end the minor Protestant sects. However, this rank order requires empirical verification as some of the Protestant sects may be far more ritualistic than at first seems apparent.

Freud, of course, likened ritualistic religion to group obsessional neurosis. The dimensional view of ritualism implies that this can be regarded as a complete explanation of the problem for only a small number of people and as Argyle (1958) pointed out, relevant evidence to the issue appears to contradict the hypothesis.

There has been very little research work attempting to link religious practices of this kind with conversion type and personality variables. Generally it is found that the more sacramental Church has a more elaborate ritual and tends to report a lower incidence of sudden conversion. It is possible that elaborate ritualistic services provide an alternative focus to the conversion experience stressed by the evangelical Churches.

Associated with most services of worship are certain related activities, namely confession, forgiveness, prayer, and praise. As volumes could be written about each one only a few brief observations will be made here.

Confession

Confession or some similar mechanism is essential for alleviating guilt, and guilt is very clearly associated with the concept of ' sin '. Sin is a term with complex meaning which has different significance for different people. For many individuals it is often connected with immorality, but theologically it is variously defined as transgression of the Law or the Will of God. (What is meant by the Law or Will of God calls for further definition.) Pragmatically such transgression normally means acting contrary to the accepted standards of a group to which one belongs. Guilt is the feeling experienced after such an act, provided one expects the consequences, either short- or long-term, to be unpleasant. These unpleasant consequences could include attitude changes towards the person by his group. One would expect high levels of guilt to be experienced by individuals belonging to groups which have a high standard of ethical and moral behaviour, and where membership of the group is highly desirable. These conditions are generally fulfilled in most Christian denominations. Confession is the means by which this guilt is eased.

Psychologically, confession works on the counselling technique employed in the treatment of neurosis. It is an opportunity for a person to talk about his problems and worries to someone else who is interested, but who will keep confidences. It is probably true to say that the counselling method was used for many centuries by the Christian Church before it was developed by Clinical Psychology. (For certain Christians confession is a very mechanical and formal affair and it is automatically followed by penance and absolution. In such circumstances there is little similarity between confession and counselling.) Sacramentally, confession is an objective sign of sincere repentance. In the case of confession practised as an element in religious life, the counsellor may be a friend, a minister, or God.

Forgiveness

This concept enables the religious person to go one stage further in his search for relief from guilt. The belief is that God forgives the sins of those who truly repent. Repentance is considered more than remorse, and includes a demand for a a ' turning away ' from sin. The repentance and plea for forgiveness may be expressed directly to God, or to some minister, or indeed to any representative of the Christian community. In the case of confession to a minister, it is followed by ' absolution ' which is a declaration by the minister on behalf of God, that repentant sinners are forgiven. This behaviour may take place in private or may be expressed by the whole group in public. This is what is found at the beginning of each of the main services of the Anglican liturgy.

Some time has been spent in discussing these two aspects of worship because of an interesting point which arises from them. While one would predict that religious people in general would have higher intensity guilt feelings than the normal population, because of the mechanism of forgiveness any actual measurement of guilt could show the religious sample less guilt-ridden than a normal population. It is interesting to note that the mechanism of forgiveness is not available to the clinical psychologist as a psychologist. If it was, his success rate of dealing with guilt feelings might be a lot higher.

Prayer

Behaviourally prayer seems to be nothing more than the partici-pant talking to himself and adopting peculiar postures to do so. Scientific observation can tell us little more about prayer; it is only when one considers the motivational aspects that prayer becomes more understandable. The motive behind prayer is belief. When it is realised that adherents firmly believe that they are talking to God and that they expect Him to answer in some way, not neces-sarily verbally, and that He demands their full allegiance and reverence, even to the extent that He makes it their duty to address Him, then the postures and the language of prayer becomes more intelligible. This illustrates the difficulty of obtaining an accurate picture from the objective measurement of behaviour, while ignor-ing the more subjective beliefs which motivate much of human behaviour.

The religious person believes that prayer is his direct access to God, and thus his prayers include confession and the plea for for-giveness, praise, intercession, supplication, and thanksgiving. There are several different types of prayer; verbal, silent, and medita-tional. The verbal, as we have already mentioned, can take place in private or in public as a group, when one person prays aloud and the others follow in silence. This is the type of prayer most often used in public worship, and in this case one person only does the speaking. At other meetings of the group for prayer, the members take it in turns to pray aloud. At the prayer meetings in some countries the members may pray their own individual prayers aloud at the same time. Although this produces a cacophony making it impossible for anyone to follow, the believers feel that it is not a problem for God. They are using a multi, as opposed to a single channel communication system!

Silent prayer is the activity of merely thinking the prayers rather than voicing them. This is normally the method used in private prayer. Meditational prayer involves concentrating deeply about an aspect of God or a story of Christ until the person is more acutely aware of God or feels that he is actually present when the particular story of Christ occurred. This is normally referred to as the practice of the Presence of God. It includes such methods as the continuous repetition of a phrase or a sentence such as 'God is love' for a period of time. It may be true to say that there is a psycho-logical, as well as a religious process at work in this type of prayer.

Praise

The glorification of God for what He is and what He has done is praise and it includes hymn singing. It is general in the more emotional sector of the religious life and occurs both in private and public worship, although it is usual to confine hymn singing to public worship. Praise of God can be directed towards others, so that they are able to share the individual's experience of God's activity, or towards God Himself. It is difficult to see why God should want a recital of His own virtues, and activities, said or sung to Him, but this is more a theological than a psychological problem. It is sufficient to note that believers think He does, and thus they indulge in this type of behaviour.

It appears that religious practices, both public and private, are motivated by the religious belief system, and that without an understanding of the beliefs underlying the behaviour they may be almost incomprehensible. Listening to a sermon (or not listening!) may be considered a religious practice, but although it takes up quite a large percentage of the total time in church it seems to serve a different purpose. The sermon is normally an attempt to stimulate thought about a certain topic in the religious field, or to admonish, or reprove, if some failure has been noticed. It acts in many ways like the group religious conscience, endeavouring to keep members up to standard. It is therefore perhaps best linked with the consequential dimension.

A simple frequency measure is used for most of these religious practices and some other, such as Bible reading, attendance at the sacraments, etc. The measurement of confession and forgiveness however may prove quite difficult unless it is institutionalised as in the Roman Catholic Church. These investigations provide useful information about the level of such activities in the general population, or in specific religious groups, but some other method of investigation is necessary to improve our understanding of the underlying processes involved in them.

RELIGIOUS FEELINGS AND EXPERIENCE

This particular area of religion should include conversion experience, mysticism and glossolalia. In general these are usually thought of as discrete variables and not dimensions and for this reason the subject was discussed in chapter 4. However, a case can be made for a continuum on the basis of the varying incidence of mystical experiences, or ecstatic utterances reported by individuals. It seems appropriate at this point, therefore, to examine mysticism and glossolalia in greater detail.

Mysticism

Mysticism can be defined as the attempt by the individual to lose his own identity and become one with the ultimate. It is not exclusively Christian, nor is it confined to the West. It is probably true to say that the Eastern civilisations have been practising mysticism for centuries longer than those of the West.

There have been several attempts by psychologists to investigate the phenomena associated with mysticism, but as the mystical experience is essentially subjective many of the tools available to the psychologist are ineffective. What has been done is an analysis of the reports of mystical experience, and a comparison of similar phenomena in other fields of psychology. The mystical experience may come to the mystic by chance or by design. In the first case, the person is seeking no such experience, but is going about his normal life when the experience takes place. St. Paul's vision and voice on the Damascus road is an example. In the second case, the experience is sought, for example by fasting, flagellations, solitude, and stringent self-denial. By whatever way they come the experiences have been traditionally divided into three classes. The first class is referred to as *exterior* visions or locutions. In such cases the object seen or heard appears to the percipient to belong to the outside world. The second may be called *imaginal*, and here the percipient has a clear image of what he sees or hears, but does not suppose it to belong to the outside world. The third is known as *intellectual* visions or locutions; in these cases the object is stated to be neither seen nor heard, but there is an inner feeling of a presence or a communication. It seems likely that most of the visions and locutions are either intellectual or imaginal, and that the exterior kind are very rare. St. Teresa, for example, records that she never had an exterior vision or locution.

One of the important features of the reported visions and locutions is the 'interpretive element'. It is inevitable that certain interpretations should be made when attempting to convey one's experiences to others, but the interpretive element might accompany the experience itself. To illustrate these two suggestions imagine a person who reports that he has had a vision of Christ. What he actually saw was a man dressed in a certain way and doing certain things, but in retrospect, because the clothing and the actions conform to the person's conception of Christ, he reports that he has experienced a vision of Christ. The vision may present no clues to the identity of the object, and yet the percipient knows that the person is Christ. This intuitive knowledge accompanies, or indeed is part of, the vision itself. Perhaps an example from dream experience will help to clarify the situation further. In a dream one might intuitively recognise a particular outline as a certain person, and yet when the form is recognisable it is not the person one 'knew' it to be. This can be very frightening and it is possible that experiences of this kind are responsible for changing dreams into nightmares. Not every experience has the interpretive element, but the vast majority do, and it is this part of the experience which gives the whole its particular significance.

Visions (the term will be used to refer to both visions and locutions) may come frequently or once in a lifetime, and not all make significant changes in subsequent behaviour. Here the interpretive element seems to be more directly linked to personality and learning; than to the actual vision. The percipient's interpretation of his vision is based in most cases on the beliefs he holds at that moment. Thus the Hindu does not see visions of Christ or the Virgin Mary, and the monk does not have visions of Hindu deities. Pantheists have visions where Nature is the subject and subsequently receives the devotion and worship.

There are visions, however, which do seem to produce significant behaviour changes. St. Paul's conversion is an outstanding example. As far as it is possible to deduce, Paul had never seen Christ in person. This is supported by the fact that his claim to apostleship was in part based on the fact that he had seen Christ ' as one born out of due time ', referring to the vision he had. But in the vision the actual identity was established, 'Who art thou Lord?', 'I am Jesus who thou persecutest'. Thus the interpretive element is coming within the vision itself. But the behaviour change might be explained in the same psychological terms used to explain conversion (see chapter 6). Conflict and tension had built up through Paul's persecution of the Church, and the vision experience was a trigger for the change of behaviour, in the same way that some words of an evangelist might bring about a similar behavioural change in one of his listeners.

When the vision itself, excluding the interpretive element, is examined, one finds striking similarities to the experiences reported by people suffering from hallucinations, and the effects of certain drugs on subjective experiences. This poses the possibility that there is a common denominator underlying the occurrence of visions. The most likely cause could be biochemical, the presence or absence of a certain chemical or chemicals producing these experiences. A temporary state could be explained by a minor malfunction of short duration; a more permanent malfunction could explain the psychotic hallucinatory experiences. Drugs, fastings, flagellations, or solitude may be methods of producing such a temporary malfunction of the brain. But it is important to recall the significance of the interpretive element in the typical religious experience. An interesting experiment in this area was conducted by Pahnke (1966). He investigated the effects of psilocybin (a psychedelic drug) on a group of theological students within a religious context. He found that the subjective experiences reported by the subjects in comparison to the control group were very similar to the reported qualities of mystical experiences. The result confirms the suggestion made earlier that the mystical experience is biochemical, or physiological in character, and its religious quality is determined by the context or previous religious experience of the individual.

It is easy to see that fasting and flagellation may produce biochemical changes similar to those induced by drugs, but there is additional evidence that some kinds of meditation can produce physiological changes. Wallace (1970) examined the physiological effects of transcendental meditation and found that there was a 20 per cent decrease in oxygen consumption and a significant increase in skin resistance. It is possible that these effects and others as yet undetected could contribute to the induction of mystical experiences.

The mystical experience is not confined to a celebrated few in the religious world. Most devout Christian people have had at some time of their life such an experience, probably of the intellectual vision or locution type. This may occur during a conversion experience, or as part of a call to a particular type of service – the ministry or the mission field – or during a time of devotion and worship. When this is realised, the question arises whether the different types of mystical experience have the same causal agents. The intellectual type seems to be only an heightened sense of awareness. But whether it is merely quantitative differences in the causal agent which produced the three different types or three distinct causes remains a subject for further research.

Glossolalia

The study of mysticism leads to an associated phenomenon, that of ecstatic speech. There has been very little systematic work on this subject, and even the Christian Church itself has, while not denying its existence, ignored it, thus granting it little significance. Until recently this has been the general attitude, but now the Pentecostal Protestant group make much of this experience, and in some circles it is required for full membership of the church. There is also evidence that the movement is spreading within the Pentecostal setting (as shown by the very rapid growth in South America), and outside of it in other denominations (for example the Episcopal Church of the United States has had a number of occurrences of the phenomenon, and recently it has occurred in certain Church of England parishes).

Ecstatic utterances, often referred to in Christian circles ' as speaking in tongues ', can be defined as ' unintelligible utterance not subject to direct control by the individual '. There are certain modifications which must be made to the definition in as much as some individuals do claim a certain amount of control, and because there are people who claim another associated ' gift of the Spirit ' called the ' interpretation of tongues ', where the utterances are translated. These ' gifts of the Spirit ' are recorded as being present in the early church. There are references to them on the Book of Acts and a fairly lengthy discussion of them by St. Paul in his first letter to the Corinthians. The name Pentecostalism comes from the original gift of the Spirit at Pentecost. The ' gifts of the Spirit ' possessed by the Pentecostalists and like-minded groups are not confined to the two already mentioned. A number of others are claimed such as those recorded in 1 Corinthians 12 ' the word of wisdom ', ' the word of knowledge ', ' faith ', ' gifts of healing ', ' working of miracles ', ' prophecy ', and ' the discerning of spirits '. There seems little doubt that the Pentecostalists do possess at least some of these gifts but perhaps an objective scientist would describe the phenomena in much more mundane language. Few, if any, objective studies have been made of these phenomena. Many people witnessing public acts of healing have considered them fakes, but no conclusive evidence has been produced either way. The close connection with mysticism seems obvious; in the one case the eyes and the ears seem to be possessed by external forces, and in the other case the tongue and lips seem similarly possessed; in both cases the subject plays a passive role.

The four characteristics of mysticism distinguished by William James (1902) are also indeed characteristic of the ecstatic utterances : ineffability, neotic quality, transiency, and passivity (see page 11). Are there any personality factors associated with mysticism and ecstatic utterances? Many would maintain there are. But at present there is little experimental evidence on the subject. The ' speaking in tongues ' experience is usually a post-conversion experience, and many who have reported such an experience have mentioned the renewed vitality that the experience brought to their existing religious life, and that each succeeding experience continues to maintain this vitality. The fact that similar experiences are reported in other non-

Christian religious or pseudo-religious groups, and that some psychotic patients have similar experiences may indicate that here again a psychological mechanism is in use and is given a religious significance. Additional support for this conclusion is provided by Cohn (1967) who was able to experimentally produce glossolalia type experiences in a laboratory setting.

There has been an increasing interest is glossolalia in the last few years as the recent book by Kildahl (1972) would indicate. The interest has come mainly from a psycholinguistic perspective. Osser et al. (1973), analysing instances of glossolalia have found two distinct types, repetitive and an innovative speech type. The latter, they feel, may indicate some measure of linguistic creativity. There is also some controversy over the significance of personality factors in glossolalia and the interpretation given to research findings in the area. A re-examination of the problem is provided by Richardson (1973).

Emotionalism

It is impossible to discuss religious feeling without some reference to the part emotions play in the religious life. The extent of their importance is dependent, in part on the personality of the individual. As the religious life demands for the devout a response from the whole organism, one would expect the emotions to be important. Worship itself, of course, is in essence an emotional activity, but in certain Christian denominations and sects the emotions seem to be stressed almost to the exclusion of other more intellectual factors. The groups who possess such 'gifts' as 'speaking in tongues' are obviously laying great stress on the emotions. There are suggestions that those who respond emotionally rather than rationally would be more at home in these surroundings.

It is necessary to make some distinction between emotionalism and emotionality. The former is used to refer to the tendency to respond to a given situation by asking 'What do I feel?', rather than 'What do I think?'. The latter is used by Eysenck in reference to emotional stability/instability and as synonymous with neuroticism. It seems likely that religious people who have a tendency to emotionalism will be members of religious groups which stress the important of emotion. There are some indications that women tend to be more emotional than men, and that the extreme Protestant group emphasises emotion in their teaching and practice. Thus the prediction can be made that there will be a larger ratio of women to men in the more extreme Protestant groups.

This is indeed what is found (Argyle 1958). Wilson (1961) made a similar conclusion; he suggested the reason for his finding of a relatively small ratio (of women to men) for Christadelphians was the lack of emotional release at the services. Here (if the above hypothesis is accepted) the interplay of personality on religious allegiance can be seen.

The opposite of emotionalism can be referred to as intellectualism, the tendency to respond to situations in a rational rather than an emotional way. The people who respond in this way would, it seems, belong to the groups where emotion is lightly stressed, such as the more formalised Protestant bodies.

If true, these hypotheses would tend to keep the character of the denomination or sect fairly constant, but there is evidence which suggests that there is a tendency for extreme and highly emotional sects to become more formalised with the passage of time, and become more orthodox institutionalised denominations with a decreased emphasis on emotion. A simple explanation for this may be a general decrease in emotionalism with increase in age, and/or the progressive lowering of the emotionalism of succeeding recruits. The emotional level of church services may also have an ethnic link. The negro churches in the U.S.A. have a far greater emotional content than their equivalent white denomination.

In addition to the more dramatic experiences that have been discussed in this section of the chapter, there is the feeling, or sense of awareness which characterises some religious people. It seems to give them an apprehension of something which is otherworldly and beyond their intellectual comprehension. It is probably related to mystical experience and could be called a dimension of mysticism. The scale would measure the individual's tendency to view religion in a mystical way, to stress the sense of awareness of the divine and even the extent he wishes to lose his own identity and unite with the divine. It would be an extremely difficult scale to devise and apply, especially as the vast majority do not seem to have, or want these experiences. Such a scale may have value for the more mystical Eastern religions. Broen's other dimension may be attempting to measure something along these lines. This dimension was unipolar and named 'nearness to God'. Those scoring high on this factor emphasise communion with God, a loving relationship with God who is always near at hand, guiding and directing. It could be described as a factor of awareness. Certain individuals are acutely aware of God's presence, while for others He is remote, merely an abstract concept. The awareness of God's presence has often been noted as one of the distinguishing marks in the lives of the Saints. In one sense this may also be a measure of relevance. A god whose presence is continually felt will influence the individual's daily decisions and thus be relevant to his life, while one who is remote does not have this affect and may therefore appear irrelevant. There is however a problem. Some people who stress the transcendence and remoteness of God, also emphasise His nearness and contact with man. The ' omni-ness' of God seems to separate Him from man while His love and care draws God and man closer together. The Christian faith contains many such paradoxes, and people may wish to hold both these views of God at the same time. There are two possible aspects if this dimension, one stressing relevance in terms of nearness or remoteness; the other stressing the character of God in similar terms. Relevance seems to be the aspect with which Broen is chiefly concerned.

Very closely related to the idea of God's nearness and relevance is a dimension dealing with the personal or impersonal attitude to religious beliefs. The religious activity of some individuals is sustained by a highly personal commitment to God or their Church. They are internally motivated. In contrast, there are people whose motives are dictated by factors not directly connected with religious faith but artifacts of the social and economic milieu surrounding religion. There people are not motivated by personal religious commitment, but by extrinsic values. The variable here is obviously measuring some type of conventionalism. The contrast Argyle (1958) makes between the genuinely devout and the conventionally religious is very similar to the person/impersonal dimensions. Tests of conventionalism and personal commitment will be measuring the the same variable.

Another important dimension which seems to be measuring the same variable is Wilson's (1960) Instrinsic/Extrinsic Scale. He again is making the distinction between solely personal religious motivation and motives which include the social/financial benefits of membership, for instance church members patronising one's business. In addition Wilson includes more sophisticated benefits which might accrue from spiritual exercises, for example, prayer as a means of securing divine protection and provision. The dimension may be more complicated than was first thought. Amon and Yela (1968) concluded from their studies that instrinsic/extrinsic religiosity was not a single dimension. They identify an intrinsic dimension which sees religious values as ends in themselves and two extrinsic dimensions, one concerned with economic and social power, the other as a style of living.

Additional work has been done in this area by Hoge (1972) who has produced a new scale of intrinsic religious motivation. It is based on a dimension of Hunt and King (1971), ultimate (intrinsic)/ instrumental (extrinsic). Another important point supporting the work of Amon and Yela concerns the two aspects of extrinsic value. There is the more outward form involving immediate materialistic concerns, such as the idea that church attendance is good for business, and the more inward type gaining specific spiritual benefits, heavenly rewards for instance.

The problem of motivation, whether it is conventional/extrinsic or intrinsic (more internal) is basically a question of commitment. It includes not only the extent of the commitment, but also the object attracting such commitment. Work by Coates (1973) looks at the extent of Roman Catholic commitment. Members of a Catholic religious order are classed as highly committed; lay members at seminaries as moderately committed; while Roman Catholic students have low commitment. He then goes on to look at various personality differences between the three groups. Hunt (1972) however looks at a different problem. He is concerned with religious meaning and the individual's commitment to certain possible interpretations. He lists three possibilities: literalism, anti-literalism, and mythological. He devises a scale to measure them, and claims that this technique is better than the fundamentalist literalist measure usually employed, because it can detect more readily sophisticated changes in approach to religious material.

Questions which ask for some estimate of how religious a person thinks he is may also be measuring internal motivation. This could account for the fairly large percentage of members of the various churches who assess themselves as 'not very religious' or 'not at all religious' (38–11 per cent) in the I.T.A. (1970) survey.

Conventionalism is a very important dimension, no matter how it is measured. It enables the investigator to ignore to some extent the complication of determining religious motives in sample selection. He can now include all those who ostensibly take part in some religious activity and relate his findings to the religious conventionalism dimension.

Religiosity has normally been a general measure of religious belief and attitude but in the I.T.A. (1970) survey it is used as a measure of the personal importance of religion to the individual. This is slightly different from the personal/impersonal continuum because the individual with extrinsic motives may feel that religion is very important to him. But an examination of the nine questions which constitute the religiosity scale seem to indicate a measure of personal religious commitment, so religiosity seems to be another measure of religious conventionalism.

TABLE 4: RELIGIOSITY SCALE ITEMS

Those who said that:	Britain %	N. Ireland %
1. They were 'very religious' or 'fairly religious'	58	75
2. They are 'certain' that to lead a good life it is necessary to have some religious belief	42	74
3. They are 'certain' that without belief in God life is meaningless	41	75
4. They are 'certain' that religion helps to maintain the standards and morals of society	55	81
5. They are 'certain there is a God'	50	86
6. They believe that 'God does watch each person'	59	86
7. They are 'very likely' to think of God when they are worried	43	72
8. They are 'very likely' or 'fairly likely' to think of God when they are happy	51	70
9. Their everyday lives are affected 'a great deal' or 'quite a lot' by their religious beliefs	46	76

(from I.T.A. 1970)

The relationship between the dimension of religious conventionalism and other factors is less clear, there has been little work done on the subject, but results so far would seem to indicate that there are significant relationships between conventionalism, authoritarianism, and prejudice.

If conventionalism is a personality variable then one would expect it to influence not only religious beliefs but also political beliefs. Scobie found that the F-Scale measure of conventionalism was very significantly correlated with both religious conservatism and political conservatism. Therefore, as one might expect, the dimension of religious conservatism and religious conventionalism are not independent. A conventional attitude in our present society is more closely linked with conservative religious beliefs. For this reason many of the relationships found to apply to religious conservatism and other factors will also hold for religious conventionalism. It seems necessary to develop measures of conservatism and conventionalism which are not correlated, or alternatively to find a single dimension or factor which is basic to them both.

One of the problems with the dimension of conventionalism is to find its correct placement within the three areas we have considered. Although we have placed it within the area of religious feelings, it could be argued that it lies within the field of religious belief where a person either believes that religion should be motivated by inner feelings or simply by practical non-religious considerations.

Again it is possible to see a link between conversion type and the measures of conventionalism, so that those individuals who have had a dramatic religious experience are more likely to be motivated by inner feelings associated with the experience. This implies that sudden and gradual converts will be more intrinsic in their religious attitudes, a subject we will examine further in chapter 7.

SUMMARY

The variables of religious belief examined in this chapter indicate the difficulties an investigating psychologist might have in finding a reliable measure of religious behaviour. It would seem necessary when any attempt to measure religion is made that the three basic dimensions of belief, practice, and experience should be used.

6

Theories of Religious Belief and Behaviour

There have been numerous suggestions about the possible causes of religion and religious belief. The main purpose of the present chapter is to examine the principal theories and then to see how successful they are in accounting for the three conversion types described in chapter 4.

THE THEORIES

A name which figures predominantly in any discussion of theories of religion is, of course, Freud (1907, 1927, 1933). His main contribution may be called a frustration theory. He suggested that religion is one way of compensating or adapting to the many frustrations of society and life in general. Man is frustrated by nature's uncontrollable storms, earthquakes, and volcanic eruptions, and by the whole process of ageing and prospective death. Freud saw the claims of society as frustrating the demands of the 'Id' by insisting on extensive control of sexual and aggressive desires. Certain men, usually the working class, are also subject to additional frustration imposed on them by society because of their class status and supposed value to the society. Freud's idea is that man, through religion, finds a substitute which compensates for his inability to overcome these frustrations of life. He develops this frustration theory further, and states that man's response to frustration is regression to the period in his life when he was dependent on his own father. Such a father may no longer be available or appropriate to his present situation, so he looks for a substitute which he finds in the concept of God. God then becomes a substitute father-figure, protecting and chastising him, acting the same way as his own father. This hypothesis caused quite a stir, implying as it did that God was no more than a fantasy father-figure, a creation of man. More recent work questions the importance of the concept of the father-figure in religious belief. An investigation using the Q-technique of sorting was conducted by Nelson and

D

Jones (1958) to study the concepts of God and Jesus in comparison with the concepts of mother and father. The technique used was to provide a number of half sentences where God, Jesus, mother or father formed the subject, for example, ' When I think of God I . . .', and subjects were required to rank in order part sentences which could be used to complete the given sentence, such as '. . . have a feeling that I am understood '. The rank order was to be based on a continuum where the complete sentence represents feelings most like those of the subject, to those feelings least like those of the subject. They tentatively concluded that diety concepts are more closely related to the mother rather than the father concept, but only 16 Protestant subjects (8 male, 8 female) were tested, so further work is necessary using a more extensive sample.

Freud has a further contribution to make to the discussion of theories of religious belief. He suggests that ritualistic religion is a group response similar to the individual response referred to as obsessional neurosis. People who suffer from this mental illness feel they are forced to act in a particular way and they devise elaborate rituals which must be adhered to in every detail or catastrophe will overtake them. Freud was quick to point out the similarity this illness has with the ritual acts and words employed in services of worship by a number of denominations or sects.

Freud was not the only person to suggest a frustration theory of religious belief. The ideas of Marx are dependent on the idea that the frustrations of the working class are reduced by religious belief and commitment. In order to release the power of the working class it is necessary to reveal and neutralise the tranquillising nature of religion.

Leuba (1925) and Thouless (1924) both postulated sexual frustration and deprivation as the basis of religion. Their evidence is based in part on what they believed to be the excessive sexual symbolism found in the writings of many mystics. Thouless also felt that the emphasis of chastity by a number of religious groups was additional evidence for the sexual origin of religion. The greater religious activity of the unmarried and the widowed in comparison with those who are married is further confirmation of the sexual frustration hypothesis although other theories may provide alternative explanations for the finding.

Another theory derived from Freud and psychoanalysis and put forward by Flugel (1945) is a conflict theory. He suggests that conflict occurs in a person between the ' super-ego ' (the conscience) and the ' id ' (the basic desires or instincts). This internal conflict is relieved by the projection mechanism. Projection is a method by which the person externalises a belief or desire and acts as if such attributes belong no longer to himself but to other people or things. It is essentially a defence mechanism for it is much easier for the individual to act in relation to externalised objects or people than to attempt to change himself. The projection mechanism is seen as a possible basis of prejudice (the scapegoat theory). The desires and impulses which the individual finds as an unacceptable and unbearable part of himself he projects onto a particular group. This group, and no longer himself, possesses these undesirable traits and he can actively condemn such people without condemning himself.

Flugel suggests that the projection mechanism transforms the universe into God and the Devil, by attributing to the first the feelings of the super-ego and to the second the feelings of the id.

A further phase of the conflict theory is centred around the concept of guilt feelings. Certain authors such as Pfister (1948) suggest that the main purpose of religion is to relieve guilt feelings. The conflict experienced by such people is not relieved by the projection mechanism, but continues to be internalised and they blame themselves for not keeping up to the standards imposed by their super-ego. This self-blame produces guilt feelings which can be relieved by religious belief and behaviour. The religious concept of divine forgiveness (see chapter 5) is of extreme importance in this context.

Another group of ideas put forward as explanations of the origin of religious belief are described by Argyle (1958) as cognitive need theories. It is suggested by such proponents that the impetus for religious belief is a desire on the part of the individual to understand or give meaning to the universe and his own personal life. Weber's (1922) suggestion that religious belief is an attempt to solve the problem of the meaning of life, is stressing the cognitive aspects of religion. Flower (1927) also produced a cognitive theory, suggesting that religion may be viewed as,

‘ essentially an attitude determined by the discrimination of an element of “ utterly-beyondness ”, brought about by a mental development which is able to appreciate the existence of more in the world than that to which existing endowment effects adequate adjustment.’ (Flower 1927, p. 30).

The implication of Flower's idea is that the religious response is one that arises as a consequence of man's willingness to entertain the possibility of more to the world than that which is readily discernible by his senses. In this way he gives meaning to those experiences which are for him inexplicable.

The social support hypothesis of Festinger (1954 and 1956) can also be applied to religious groups. Festinger maintains that beliefs, opinions, abilities, etc., need to be evaluated by the individual. In many cases there are practical tests which can be applied to verify such beliefs, but there are, however, numerous opinions which are not amenable to empirical verification. When this occurs evaluation is made on the basis of comparison with other people; if there is no such evaluation then opinions and beliefs become unstable. Religious beliefs are of course not amenable to empirical or scientific verification and in order to maintain such beliefs it is necessary to compare them with the beliefs of other people. In other words, social support may be necessary to maintain beliefs which are difficult or impossible to prove. Festinger also suggests that the evaluative process is only possible when the abilities and opinions of the other individuals are fairly close to those expressed by the person concerned. Such a person is more likely to be attracted by a group of people who have similar opinions and abilities, which implies that the religious person joins a group which has similar beliefs to his, and derives social support for his beliefs by belonging to the group.

Brown (1962), in his factor analytic studies, has provided additional support for a cognitive system. In consequence of his discovery of the possible independence of religious belief from other personality factors, he concludes that religious belief is a 'cognitive system requiring strong social support for its maintenance'.

Social culture and tradition are learnt from the preceding generations and passed onto the next, thus ensuring a relative constancy of behaviour within a particular society. It has often been assumed that religious beliefs are transmitted in a similar way. The perpetuation of a religion in a particular country had led to particular religions being associated with such countries. This phenomenon confirms what may be called the social learning theory, which is widely held and probably would be the most acceptable explanation of religious belief for the religious community at large.

Jung's contribution to the psychology of religion has been great, but diffuse. In consequence it is difficult to present his formulation in a way which does justice to his efforts to understand religion. He emphasises the experiential character of religion rather than its theological or academic aspects. By religion Jung means an experience, not a creed. He emphasises psychic reality or what God or religion means within the individual and not some abstract or absolute concept which is outside of the person and his psyche.

No reference can be made to Jung without referring to his concept of 'archetype'. The archetypes are constituent parts of the collective unconscious which determine the symbolic reason that man uses in an attempt to express his reaction to what he comprehends as essentially mysterious or other-worldly. The term 'collective unconscious' has also a distinctive Jungian significance. He supports the contention that man is not only born with a built-in or genetical capacity for certain physical responses, but he also has a genetical or inherited psychological, or psychical capacity. The quality and character of man's brain is derived and developed through a long line of ancestors whereas the collective or racial unconsciousness is that part of man's psychical nature which is common to all men and forms part of his inherited characteristics. It is, then, the psychical, as opposed to the physical, characteristics which are common to all men. For Jung, God is an archetype and in this way influences many of man's responses. To consider God an archetype is not to claim that the concept of God is merely a creation of the mind. Jung (1953) points out that archetypes are imprints, and that imprints presuppose a printer. He maintains that the religious and theological viewpoints are concerned with the imprinter, while psychology exclusively investigates the imprint. It would be a mistake to claim that Jung had produced a theory of the origin of religious belief. His writings imply a system rather than a theory, a system in which religion and religious belief form an integral part; but unfortunately the nature of his system makes it extremely difficult to test scientifically.

There have been some attempts to provide physiological explanations of religious belief, but with the possible exception of Sargant these attempts have rarely reached an adequate or formal presentation of religious behaviour. Certain effects brought about by drugs or psychosis can often have a religious content, but whether this reveals any physiological predisposition to religion is a matter for conjecture, and it would seem more probable that investigations in this area will produce greater understanding of drugs and psychosis, rather than of religious belief and behaviour. The attempt to link religious experience with sexuality is somewhat limited in its scope. For example Leuba's (1925) suggestion that the religious ecstasies of female mystics were sexual orgasms derived by continuous contemplation of male saints or other religious figures, at best has a very restricted application.

In his book *Battle for the Mind* Sargant (1957) applies Pavlovian concepts of conditioning, excitation and inhibition to the conversion experience.

Pavlov (1972) in some of his experiments with dogs investigated 'mental breakdown'. He found that if the dog's nervous system is subjected to long period of trans-marginal stimulation – stimulation beyond the capacity for normal response – then eventually the responses become inhibited. This reaction results in altered behaviour and affords the animal's nervous system some protection. He refers to the decrease in response as trans-marginal inhibition and describes three distinct phases :

(1) The 'equivalent phase' where the brain gives the same response to strong and weak stimuli;
(2) The 'paradoxical phase' where the brain responds more actively to weak stimuli than to strong;
(3) The 'ultra-paradoxical phase' in which the conditioned reponses and behaviour patterns turn from positive to negative, or from negative to positive.

In addition to these responses there may also occur under these circumstances a state of brain activity similar to hysteria in man.

Another accidental discovery of Pavlov is important. At one point the life of his dogs was threatened by flood water, and in order to be saved, they had to be pulled under the water and out through the door of the room into the corridor. This was a most terrifying experience for the dogs, and in consequence all their learned conditioned reflexes were disrupted. Therefore, it was concluded that stress beyond levels experienced in trans-marginal inhibition produced further inhibitory activity in which all the recently implanted conditioned reflexes were temporarily forgotten.

Sargant attempted to apply Pavlov's findings to human activity and in particular to religious conversion. He states,

The subject must first have his emotions worked upon until he reaches an abnormal condition of anger, fear, or exaltation. If this condition is maintained or intensified by one means or other hysteria may supervene, whereupon the subjects can become more open to suggestion, which in normal circumstances he summarily rejected. Alternatively the equivalent paradoxical or ultra-paradoxical phases may occur. Or a sudden complete inhibitory collapse may bring about a suppression of previously held belief and behaviour patterns (Sargant, 1957).

He maintains that a similar response is precipitated in the treatment of mental disorder. The brain is subjected to abnormally high levels of stimulation and stress by the use of drugs or electric shock. This results in collapse with the possible total inhibition of recently acquired abnormal behaviour patterns. During this period of possible behavioural vacuum, new and healthy patterns of behaviour may be implanted into the brain, by the psychotherapeutic efforts of the psychiatric team.

Sargant's conclusion is that conversion is a type of brain-washing in which the brain is subjected to great stress until either all previously held beliefs have been cleared or the individual is made susceptible to new suggestions.

Weber, Durkheim and others have offered some sociological explanations of religion in which religion is seen in relation to its importance for the maintenance of society. A further discussion of the work of sociologists on religion will be found in chapter 8. One could also describe Marx's idea of the interplay of religion and social class and his description of religion as the opium of the people as a sociological explanation.

Most of the theories of the origin of religion referred to here have been described in greater detail by Argyle (1958). He makes an assessment of their value and applicability in terms of the number of statistical findings they explain. He also points out their main inadequacies in these same terms. He generally favours the conflict theory with its two aspects of projection and guilt feeling reduction.

The principle inadequacy of each of these theories is that it treats religious belief and behaviour in an oversimplified way. Each assumes that one or two variables are adequate to describe all the phenomena associated with religion. More recent work emphasises the multi-dimensional character of religious belief. A complex interplay of factors may be necessary to adequately account for religious behaviour.

PSYCHOLOGICAL AND PHYSIOLOGICAL EXPLANATIONS OF CONVERSION

The theories of religious belief have been discussed earlier in the chapter, so it is now appropriate to ask how successful these explanations are in accounting for the three types of conversion experience that have been identified. Some of the theories, such as the Jungian, do not produce easily testable predictions and therefore, they are not particularly helpful in this situation.

In the process described as unconscious conversion, a child brought up in a Christian home gradually comes to accept the beliefs of his parents and follows their example or that of church members. There is a marked absence of religious or moral conflict in the majority of such cases. The lack of significant conflict was probably one of the reasons James referred to them as the healthy minded. There are at least two or three possible reasons why there is an absence of conflict. First, their religious beliefs may not be particularly important to them, religion being merely a social event so that they are conventionally religious and have little, or no personal commitment to religious faith. Second, their view of God may still be the same as in childhood. They have encountered no significant traumatic experience which has challenged this view of God and so it persists unchanged and undisturbed. A third possibility describes the ideal development in which the individual's concept of God has developed in step with his physical and mental growth so that 'God' has always filled an actual and present need for the person throughout his life. There has been no conflict caused by a childhood concept of God trying to fulfil the needs of an adult.

The three alternatives suggested provide no evidence that conflict, frustration, cognitive need, or physiological change is a significant factor in unconscious conversion. The only theory which appears to be relevant is the social learning theory.

The gradual convert provides a very different picture. The childhood faith (if there was one) has been questioned and probably rejected, so that while the individual has developed mentally and physically his concept of God has remained unchanged, seemingly having little relevance to the demands of every day life. He may be experiencing conflict, frustration, or be searching for purpose and meaning in a number of areas, or perhaps one specific issue is of prime importance. For example, there may be conflict and tension about being disloyal to parents and upbringing; or, frustration may be a response to illness and thoughts of inevitable death; or, the individual may be seeking an adequate explanation for the death of a loved one. All these are possible sources of disturbance, and there are of course many more. The individual who once held a childhood faith may be continually assailed by the thought that these beliefs were fundamentally correct and he was mistaken to reject them.

The problems faced by the gradual convert need to be solved. Some potential converts have to solve a succession of issues, while others may face one central problem and its resolution brings the conversion process to a close. Certain traumatic events in the life of an individual may contribute to the beginning or development of the conversion process, as when the death of a loved one causes him to consider the problem of the ultimate purpose of life. The gradual conversion process may continue for any length of time, sometimes throughout the person's entire life. Occasionally some crisis may occur in the individual's experience which may bring the process to an end, but often the process is simply a gradual development of religious belief and commitment. However, the gradual conversion process may not always lead to religious belief. The consideration of religious problems may persuade the individual that religious belief is unjustifiable and so the gradual process may end in unbelief. In such cases it is not normally thought of as a conversion experience, although the process is very similar.

By using the concept of conflict or frustration, in these particular circumstances a fairly adequate explanation of gradual conversion can be made. The cognitive need theory alone is insufficient to provide the necessary motivating power needed to achieve the final result. The tendency is to consider the search for meaning in life to be a consequence of feelings of frustration caused by the lack of meaning, or the absence of satisfying explanations. It is very likely that conflict, frustration and cognitive need all combine to produce the gradual convert.

The sudden conversion process is perhaps the most complex of the three. The person who has this type of experience is normally not consciously aware of any great deliberation upon theological topics, nor is there any significant conflict over religious and moral issues. Then, quite suddenly, when these issues are brought to his attention, something dramatic occurs which transforms the whole tenor of his life. The transformation of his attitudes and beliefs often result in a significant behaviour change. The occasion of change may vary from a sudden traumatic experience accompanied by great emotional and hysterical manifestations, to a sudden decision lacking any significant emotional overtones.

In order to explain sudden conversion in psychological terms theorists have suggested that conflict and frustration are repressed into the unconscious. This could explain the astonishing reversal of beliefs witnessed in sudden conversions and the relief from unconscious tension could amount for the feelings of elation, joy, and emotional release experienced on such occasions. The repression of conflict and frustration does seem inadequate however, when an explanation is required for the more extreme events recorded at some of the meetings addressed by evangelists like John Wesley. The barking, screaming, swooning, fainting and convulsions of every description seem an excessive response to repressed conflict and frustration. There is another problem for the proponents of this theory : how can the idea of conflicts and frustrations repressed into the unconscious be verified? There is no obvious answer. Some sudden converts report, in retrospect, that there may have been some contemplation of religious and moral issues prior to conversion, but apart from this evidence the hypothesis remains virtually untestable.

Sargant's physiological explanation seems most appropriate for the extreme emotional responses referred to above. Additional evidence is provided by the fact that most sudden conversions of this nature occur at public meetings, where a very high level of stimulation has taken place, and where every opportunity is taken to increase the emotional level of the subjects, for example the American snake-handling cult referred to by Sargant where the participants pass poisonous snakes from one person to another. In order to deal adequately with the sudden conversion experience, it seems necessary to postulate two sub-types: one where psychological explanations may be appropriate and another in which Sargant's physiological theory may provide a deeper understanding of the phenomenon. The general distrust of intense emotional responses in Western culture seems to have significantly reduced the number of extreme sudden conversion experiences reported. Scobie (1967) found no evidence that any of his thirty-four sudden converts had experienced any of these hysterical symptoms. In churches like the Pentecostal which stress the importance of glossolalia, and in racial and cultural groups where emotional expression is more acceptable such as Southern Negro Baptist churches, the incidence of extreme sudden conversion may be very much higher.

The psychological and physiological mechanisms of conversion are not confined to one religion, or only to religious beliefs; they have general application to all types of belief systems. It is necessary, therefore, to point out the distinctive features of religious conversion. The content of a conversion experience is responsible for its individuality, and involves a large variety of religious beliefs. The content of political conversions have perhaps a similar variety of political beliefs. Ferm (1959), in his attempt to establish the uniqueness of the evangelical crisis, sudden conversion, insists on the importance of content. It is *what* is believed that is of prime significance in the discussion. The importance of the content of belief in conversion re-emphasises the psychological or physiological character of the conversion mechanism. The evangelist is utilising the psychological and physiological nature of man to engender faith. It is only the content of the conversion experience which provides the religious significance. This does not mean that all Christians stress the importance of content; many mystics, in particular, seem to have been more concerned with the experience itself than its content. This is equally true of the glossolalia experience; those churches who require it for membership seem to be more concerned with the experience than the content.

As far as can be ascertained, it is within Christianity that the religious use of the psychological mechanism of conversion is most prominent. In other areas its use seems no more than coincidental. Most cases of conversion where moral transformations and the emotion of joy are experienced, are predominantly Christian in content. It is probably true, as Ferm suggests, that this characteristic of Christian conversion can be attributed solely to the distinctive beliefs which form the content of the conversions.

When an attempt is made to compare sudden and gradual conversion (leaving aside the extremes of the sudden conversion group), they seem very similar. The main difference, as we have already observed, seems to be one of time. Sudden conversion apparently takes place in a few minutes, while gradual conversion may take years. The actual content of both types of conversion experience are very similar. The issues that the gradual convert may spend weeks or months considering, are drawn to the attention of the sudden convert by the evangelist. This becomes apparent when the evangelist's technique is examined. In most cases he spends about two-thirds of his speaking time talking about the conditions and needs of man. These range from sinfulness, (a very popular topic in extreme Protestantism) or loneliness, to the fear of illness, and death. All these issues and a number of others are of vital interest to the gradual convert. The evangelist may deal with each of these topics in a single address, or he may concentrate on one. For any listener who may have realised before the address that these conditions apply to him, the words of the evangelist become highly relevant. In most cases, however, sudden converts report neither prior thought, nor recognition of these conditions, nor the significance of the religious solution. It would seem that the evangelist has considerable preparatory work to do in his address. His main purpose is to persuade the listener that he is in a particular condition and has certain basic needs which require fulfilment. The man or woman must be shown that he is a sinner before forgiveness becomes a need, that he is basically lonely before friendship becomes a need, that his life is purposeless before there is a need for purpose, that he is afraid of death before there is a necessity for such fear to be relieved. When the evangelist has got his listeners to this point, he is in a position to pronounce the cure, ' that Christ is the answer to all our needs '. The success the evangelist has with the potential sudden convert will depend on his ability to make his listeners feel that the needs he describes are relevant to them and that the cure he offers is both available and desirable. The higher frequency of sudden conversion during times of economic depression may be explained by reference to the technique of the evangelist. In an affluent society material possessions can often become substitutes for spiritual needs and it would therefore take a more talented evangelist to depose the substitute and reveal the basic needs. Again we are getting an indication of the importance of content even in sudden conversion. The convert is made to feel the needs and avail himself of the cure in a few minutes, whereas the gradual convert is consciously considering such needs, but may take years to find the remedy for them. In this sense the sudden convert is being spoon-fed by the evangelist. This is not to deny that some people are more susceptible to psychological conversion than others; it merely underlies the similarity in content of these two types of conversion.

SUMMARY

In this chapter we have examined most of the theories of religious belief and behaviour. Each theory seems to be able to explain certain of the experimental findings but none of them appears capable of explaining all the empirical evidence. It the latter part of the chapter we examine the various conversion types and see which theories offer the best explanation for these experiences. It would appear from this chapter that a theory combining several of the hypotheses suggested by various investigators is necessary to produce an adequate explanation of religion.

Psychological Factors associated with Religious Behaviour

The study of religion using factor analysis reviewed in chapter 5 indicates how many different variables are important in religious behaviour. In this chapter some of the main psychological factors will be discussed.

SEX

Religious beliefs seem to be influenced by the sex of the individual. On all measures of religious belief women seem to score much higher than men. This fact is best illustrated by church attendance. All Christian denominations with the exception of the Eastern Orthodox Church have a greater proportion, not only of women members but of women attending the churches. Private prayer seems to be the area where there is the greatest difference. Almost twice as many women as men pray daily. This appears to be the case in Britain and the U.S.A. The most recent British survey (I.T.A. 1970) found that 1.5 as many women as men are certain there is a god, and a slightly lower proportion (1.4–1) gain a high or very high score on religiosity (the personal importance of religion to the individual).

TABLE 5: RELIGIOUS ATTITUDES, SEX, AND SOCIAL CLASS

	Total:	Sex:		Age:					
		Men	Women	16–24	25–34	35–44	45–54	55–64	65+
Religiosity	%	%	%	%	%	%	%	%	%
+ +, +	49	39	58	36	37	41	50	64	61
— —, —	51	61	42	64	63	59	50	36	39
Belief in God									
Certain	50	41	57	37	40	46	48	60	62
Uncertain etc.	50	59	43	63	60	54	52	40	38

| | * Social Class: | | | |
| | AB | C1 | C2 | DE |
Religiosity	%	%	%	%
+ +, +	53	49	47	51
— —, —	47	51	53	49
Belief in God				
Certain	44	58	47	51
Uncertain	56	42	53	49

(from I.T.A. 1970).

The basic problem is to determine the reasons for these differences. Argyle (1958) suggests that the guilt feeling version of the conflict theory is best able to explain these differences in activity. Women have more guilt feelings than men which could explain the higher proportion of women in churches that stress sin and invoke God's salvation through Christ, compared with those of a more catholic disposition which emphasise the sacramental aspects of religious life. Guilt feelings derive from internalised processes; if women are more frequently motivated by such processes then they should indulge in private prayer (also internally motivated) more often than men. Conflict theory can explain two important variables, but religious belief is so complex that it should not be presumed that the conflict theory adequately explains the religious activity of every woman. Sexual attraction may be an important factor. Most church services are conducted by men, which may make the whole situation more attractive to women. If females were responsible for all church services then more men might be encouraged to attend them. Church Youth Clubs have provided a socially acceptable means (especially for more conservative parents), for young girls to meet members of the opposite sex. In fact many clubs have provided a useful service as a marriage bureau! Such clubs normally attract a greater proportion of girls, possibly because parents are less restricting on their sons' behaviour. In recent years the restrictions placed on adolescents have been much reduced; therefore this explanation may be less relevant today. However, once these girls have become attached to a church their allegiance may persist throughout their lives. At the other end of the scale the older spinsters and widows have some difficulty in finding places for meeting other people, especially men. The church activities provide numerous opportunities for such contact. The masculine and feminine roles in our society are still quite distinct. Many of the so-called female virtues such as patience and tenderness are also stressed in the Christian ethic. Therefore, the cultural role-training of the female may make religion more attractive and acceptable to them. The higher scores on feminism that religious males gain in comparison to non-religious males is probably caused by the inclusion of positive attitudes to religion within the feminism scale. If, when allowance is made for this, differences still exist, it may indicate that the Christian way of life has greater affinity with the female role in our society. The present trend in Western culture of minimising role differences between the sexes may result in changes in the proportion of males and females who hold religious beliefs.

Sex difference in religious belief and behaviour are well established, but what causes these differences is difficult to determine. It could be the physical and personality characteristics peculiar to sex. Another possibility is that there are different opportunities for religious behaviour afforded to each sex, or the role that each sex plays in society could also contribute to differences in religious activity. But the most likely explanation is that all three contribute to the recorded differences in behaviour.

SUGGESTIBILITY

There has been some attempt to link the phenomenon of sudden conversion with suggestibility. Several investigators (Coe 1916 and Howells 1928) have found that religious conservatives and sudden converts are more suggestible. Indeed it has been shown that if conversion is required or highly valued by the individual's Church, then he is more likely to have such an experience. Clark (1949) supplies statistics comparing the number of conversions reported by sacramental churches and those reported by churches of a more evangelical nature. He found that the evangelical churches reported a significantly higher number of conversions. There is, of course, one possible limitation to the finding; that is, the reluctance of the more sacramental churches to use the term conversion to describe their particular experience. The suggestion has already been made that conversion experiences may occur in such churches but that the event is described in such terms as 'religious awakening', or 'enlightenment'.

Suggestion probably does play some part in conversion and probably a significant part in sudden conversion. The hysterical symptoms which accompany the extreme sudden converts' experience may indicate that possession of a suggestibility trait may facilitate the sudden conversion experience, although the link between suggestibility, hysteria, and extreme sudden conversion is not firmly established. The finding of Brown and Lowe (1951) that a group of Bible students scored high on the M.M.P.I. Hysteria Scale does support the hypothesis. Such Bible students, because of the evangelical approach of their church are more likely to be sudden converts. Some researchers drew analogies between conversion and hypnosis (suggestion trances). For example, Gibbon and De Jarnett (1972) maintain that sudden conversion and similar experiences are in reality 'hypnotic' phenomena, a response to implicit or explicit suggestion conveyed by the speaker or the atmosphere of the meeting, rather than the usual formal induction. As so little is understood about hypnosis it is doubtful whether anything is gained by comparing the two processes.

Suggestibility may be an important factor in sudden conversion, but it may also be significant in maintaining or modifying religious beliefs. Eysenck (1947) has distinguished three main types of suggestibility which he calls primary, secondary, and prestige suggestion. The first is demonstrated when a person carries out some motor movement suggested by the experimenter of which he may not even be aware. An example of this type of suggestibility is body sway. An individual is asked to stand upright with his eyes closed. The experimenter then suggests that his body is swaying backwards and forwards. After several minutes those high in primary suggestibility begin to sway following the movements dictated by the experimenter. Some subjects even fall over and need to be held to prevent them from injuring themselves. Religious conservatives seem to be high on primary suggestibility according to Howells (1928) and Sinclair (1928).

The second type of suggestion occurs when people perceive or recall things which are suggested by the experimenter. In ambiguous or complex situations certain individuals will perceive things merely on the basis of the experimenter's words, even when there is nothing to see at all. Similarly, with tests involving the recall of complex material, a person may report a certain object, or remember seeing a particular action, again on the basis of suggestion. The particular phrasing of a question may imply a certain answer and this is another way in which secondary suggestion could operate. The legal profession is well aware of this phenomenon and counsels object to this type of questioning. However, there is no experimental evidence as yet which links religious belief and secondary suggestion.

Prestige suggestion has been shown to have a link with religious belief. Individuals susceptible to this type of suggestion modify their opinions to bring them in line with that of a prestige person, one who is held in high esteem by them. The research of Burtt and Falkenburg (1941) and Brown and Pallant (1962) indicate that religious people respond to prestige suggestibility. But as the whole concept of conformity to group norms may be based on prestige suggestibility this type of suggestion may well be a general characteristic and not specificially related to religious belief. Differences in prestige suggestibility occur not only between members of the general population, but also within the religious population. Hence, Symington (1935) and Dreger (1952) found that religious conservatives were more suggestible than religious liberals.

This link between suggestibility and religious belief could imply that the character of religious concepts is such that only people who are willing to accept uncritically the assertion of others will become religious. The great need that religious people have for social support in order to maintain their beliefs would seem to confirm this claim. However, there are a number of very suggestible people who are not religious. We find a number of customs, traditions, and group activities of a non-religious character that seem to be maintained by the same mechanism. The conclusion one reaches is that suggestibility is only one factor among many which plays a part in the establishment and maintenance of religious belief. It is possible that the normal dynamics of group activity and not some separate, or specific mechanism is responsible for the correlation between suggestibility and religious belief.

PREJUDICE

Ethnocentrism, or racial prejudice, has been found by many investigators to correlate with religious belief. Allport and Kramer (1946) were among the first to discover this relationship. Their particular finding was a high correlation between anti-Negro prejudice and religious affiliation. There were however, denominational differences. Jews and non-religious individuals were the least prejudiced; Protestants scores were more so; while Roman Catholics had the highest prejudice score.

This was an interesting and perhaps surprising result especially in view of the stress Christian teaching places on the importance of tolerance, and the brotherhood of man. It was probably this finding more than any other which contributed to the investigation of the intra-group differences which classifies religious people in terms of frequency of church attendance, extrinsic/intrinsic religious values, etc. The finding of Kelly et al. (1958) that the relationship between prejudice and church attendance was curvilinear confirmed many previous findings, that the genuinely devout were less prejudiced than the conventionally religious. Wilson's (1960) finding of a significant correlation between anti-semitism and extrinsic religious value underlined this distinction between genuine and conventional religious values and beliefs. These investigations again emphasise the multiplicity of factors which determine participation in religious activities. The motivation of the conventionally religious seems to be quite different from that of the genuinely devout, or internally orientated religious group. Photiadis et al. (1962) shed further light on the problem. They found that church participation reduced prejudice but religious orthodoxy seems to increase it. The mellowing effect of church participation seems to operate regardless of content of belief, education or the individual's personality. In the light of the importance of church participation the information indicating differences in prejudice between denominations ought to be examined more closely. The conflicting evidence nominating either Roman Catholics or Protestants as the most prejudiced group may be attributed to variations in church participation within the samples examined. The geographical differences of prejudice for the same denominational group may indicate variations in the level of church activity for various localities. There may also be differences between new and older more well-established denominations. Strickland and Wedell (1972) maintain that the intrinsic/extrinsic dimension is only an appropriate indicator of prejudice for the more traditional religious groups such as Baptists. They found that Unitarians were more extrinsic but less prejudiced and dogmatic than Southern Baptists. Hoge and Carrol (1973) take the issue even further. They matched groups of Presbyterians and Methodists from both Northern and Southern states of America, and found that anti-Negro prejudice, but not anti-semitism was associated with religious orthodoxy and ethicalism. They suggest that the strongest determinant of prejudice was personality rather than religious factors, such as the extrinsic/intrinsic dimension. The work however needs further confirmation, for Matlock (1973) found that anti-Negro prejudice was correlated with belief in free will, extrinsic religious orientation, orthodoxy, and denominational allegiance. The picture is confused and still leaves the basic question unanswered: why should the conventionally religious be so prejudiced? There seems no simple explanation. It is possible that these people are more interested in preserving the institution to which they belong, rather than the religious values which it advocates. Any other group with alternative standards either of religious beliefs, or social/racial behaviour represents a threat to the group they support. In this way they develop negative attitudes towards such groups. It is equally possible that ethnocentrism derives from a more basic attitude or personality variable, such as authoritarianism and dogmatism, and that people with these personality traits are attracted by religion.

AUTHORITARIANISM

The discussion of ethnocentrism leads on directly to a consideration of authoritarianism, since these two variables are highly correlated. The interest in authoritarianism began with the publication of *The Authoritarian Personality* by Adorno et al. (1950). The investigation started as a study of anti-semitism. The authors devised a questionnaire scale which would measure anti-semitic attitudes. Their next step was to devise a scale for measuring all types of racial prejudice. This they named the Ethnocentrism Scale. A scale for measuring political and economic conservatism was devised and it was found that all three scales were significantly related (positive correlations were found ranging from .43 – .76). The aim of the authors was now to produce a scale which would measure the basic personality characteristics underlying the attitudes but to avoid any direct questions relating to race or politics. The scale they produced to do this was the F-scale which was purported to measure authoritarianism. They next investigated other personality characteristics which individuals scoring high on authoritarianism seem to possess. It appears that authoritarian personalities repress unacceptable impulses in themselves and project them onto other people, especially those who represent some possible or imagined threat to their own well-being. It addition they are more conformist and are more concerned with power and control rather than love and affection in human relationships. Authoritarianism also has a relationship with religious affiliation. Roman Catholics and members of the major Protestant denominations score highest on the F-scale, while Jews and the Protestant sects score much lower. But in general it seemed that religious people were more authoritarian than non-religious people. Research has revealed that authoritarianism is not a single factor, but is measuring a number of variables. Rokeach (1960) in particular has been critical of the concept, maintaining that it has biases against political conservatives. He produced an alternative scale purporting to measure dogmatism in which he defined his concept of 'close-mindedness', acceptance of proof by authority and intolerance of people who hold different beliefs or ideas. Rokeach was attempting to produce a scale which was not biased against political conservatives, but was more a measure of the way beliefs are held rather than the content of such beliefs. He demonstrated the validity of his scale by showing that in British politics the Conservative Party and the Communist Party are the most dogmatic, while the other parties fall between these two extremes and are therefore rated as less dogmatic. A considerable number of investigators using the Authoritarian F-scale have indicated that religious people in general, and religious conservatives in particular, are more authoritarian than the general population (Rhodes 1960). There is a significant correlation between authoritarianism and ethnocentrism which raises the problem whether authoritarian measures are indicating anything other than ethnocentrism. Many investigators would probably conclude that authoritarianism was measuring something more than racial prejudice. But it is also necessary to bear in mind the objection of Rokeach about its bias against political conservatives. Perhaps it is measuring a combination of both racial prejudice and political conservatism. Scobie (1967) calculated a second-order partial coefficient of correlation between authoritarianism and religious conservatism with both political conservatism and ethnocentrism kept constant. The value of .22 which he obtained is just significant at the .01 level of confidence which implies that authoritarianism is measuring something in addition to prejudice and political conservatism. The nature of this other factor is difficult to determine. It may be connected with the authoritarian's supposed use of projection or his conformity. Alternatively it may be a measure of what Rokeach has called dogmatism, the close-mindedness of the authoritarian personality. This seems the most likely explanation, especially as Rokeach was attempting to measure a similar personality variable to authoritarianism, but independent of political conservatism, although Rokeach claims that dogmatism and authoritarianism are relatively independent. Numerous studies have been produced using Rokeach's Dogmatism Scale, in which religious people seem to score high on dogmatism, especially those with fundamentalist beliefs (Stanley 1963). A more recent study by Gilmore (1969) has indicated that not all fundamentalists in the Pentecostal Church score high on the Dogmatism Scale. Low scorers seem to have personality traits which are similar to the general population rather than to the dogmatic minority. It would seem from this finding that dogmatism is not directly related to the content of beliefs. Previous results may have been due to the fact that the experimenters used too small a group of fundamentalist believers. High positive correlations have been found between dogmatism and strength or importance of religion (Di Guiseppe 1971), church attendance (Steininger et al. 1972), and consensual religiosity (Raschken 1973). But why should certain religious people be dogmatic? Dogmatism, or close-mindedness in the Rokeachian sense means an acceptance of proof by authority and an intolerance of people who hold different beliefs or ideas. Religious beliefs are outside the scope of logical proof; they cannot be empirically verified. The most one can do to justify such beliefs is to show that they are not beyond the bounds of possibility. Many religious people maintain that doctrine or theological truth is divinely revealed and not logically deduced; they accept proof by authority, divine authority, for in this case there appears to be no alternative. In a sense then, by defining dogmatism as acceptance of proof by authority, some religious people are being included simply on this basis. The intolerance of people with different ideas should not necessarily be linked with the ' accept-ance of authority', aspect of definition. Intolerance is probably related to the finding of Thouless (1935) that items of religious belief are held more intensely than items of fact. If one argues that increased intensity is a compensation for the lack of logical proof for religious concepts, then intolerance may be the natural response to the frustrations of being unable to logically justify beliefs, which the person holds as extremely important. Equally likely is the same explanation put forward for ethnocentrism, namely that any opposition poses a threat to beliefs which are difficult to justify and need to be maintained by social support. It is important to note the possibility that this aspect of Rokeachian dogmatism is merely a measure of ethnocentrism, an artifact of the scale. It is possible that whereas authoritarianism also measures both political conservatism and ethnocentrism, dogmatism, while largely inde-pendent of conservatism, is still closely connected with ethno-centrism.

An interesting recent discovery by Kilpatrick, Sutker and Sutker (1970) was the relationship between dogmatism and locality. While comparing Roman Catholic, Protestant, and Jewish scores on Rokeach's Dogmatism Scale for subjects in some Southern universi-ties of the U.S.A., they found in contrast to the Northern situation, Catholics were less dogmatic than Protestants. However, when they compared these results with those of denominations in the North, they found the Catholics had similar scores. But Southern Protestants were very much more dogmatic than their Northern equivalents. This may be a factor of the social and cultural background, or it may be related to the composition of the Protestant block in the South. These are predominantly conservative denomination groups, whereas Northern Protestants are mostly Episcopalians or Presbyterians holding a more radical approach.

INTELLIGENCE

Intelligence seems to be another important factor in religious belief. There has been a considerable amount of research into the intelligence of religious people. Two main methods have normally been used : the administration of intelligence tests and an attempt to assess the individual's success in his occupation (Fry's (1933) measure of denominational over-representation in *Who's Who*). Most intelligence test work has been done on children and students. The data collected seems to indicate that the more intelligent children are capable of understanding the meaning and significance of religious concepts earlier than their less gifted peers; but they also begin to question and doubt such beliefs at an earlier age. As students they are more likely to hold radical and unorthodox beliefs than the general population.

In general a negative correlation has been found between intelligence and religious belief (Carlson 1934, Brown and Lowe 1951) but there are some exceptions which could indicate the importance of other factors such as social conditions. The most significant relationship seems to be between intelligence and religious conservatism, the more conservative being less intelligent (Howells 1928, Symington 1935, Brown and Lowe 1951). Scobie did not find any significant relationship between the two variables but this is probably a reflection of the unrepresentative nature of his sample in terms of intellectual ability.

In America there is a significant relationship between the amount of schooling a person receives and their religious activity. A greater percentage of those who reached college level in their education claim weekly attendance at church. Some similar relationship may hold in Britain but it seems to be in the opposite direction. Those individuals who have had a secondary education seem less religious than those who have not.

The basic problem is to determine the cause of the apparent lower intelligence of religious people. One possible explanation is that religious activity demands a certain degree of conformity. Intelligent people are less inclined to accept beliefs and behaviour simply on the basis of other people's experience but demand a critical examination and evaluation of the subject matter. They are, therefore, in general less conformist in their approach to life and for this reason are perhaps less likely to approve of the somewhat restricting limitation religion might put on their activities. The finding that the more intelligent seem to be more radical and unorthodox in their beliefs would seem to give limited confirmation to the suggestion.

It would be interesting to determine the composition of intelligence levels within the religious group. The religious group may not be normally distributed like the general population. There may be a bimodal distribution based on the possible leader/follower composition of the Churches. The leadership may be highly intelligent (cf. Pratt 1937 : I.Q. values of each denomination for a student sample) whereas the followers may be far less intelligent. The clerical/lay distinction might discourage lay-leadership and this could result in the under-representation of the middle intelligence group. This must remain conjecture until further experimental verification has been carried out. However, Pratt's work seems to indicate evidence of the presence of highly intelligent individuals within the Church. If there is a lower average intelligence score for religious people then there could be over- and under-representation at some point along the intelligence continuum.

The emphasis and the interest of a particular denomination seems to affect the occupation of its members. It either discourages its younger followers from choosing particular careers or it fails to attract members of certain occupations. For example, scientists seem to be predominantly Protestant and only a comparatively small number of them are Roman Catholic. Catholics seem to prefer to be actors, artists, or politicians; while Unitarians seem to produce a relatively large proportion of natural scientists and social workers (Fry 1933).

NEUROTICISM

A consideration of the emotional character of many sudden conversion experiences leads to implications in the area of personality. Eysenck (1947, 1953) and others have seen the emotional response level as a personality variable. Some individuals always seem to respond to stimulation with high emotion, while others seem to be quite placid. This personality variable has been called neuroticism, or emotional stability. The implication is that the individuals who normally respond with high emotion will be more likely to respond in circumstances where evangelistic techniques are being employed. In other words, sudden converts will score high in neuroticism scales. There is some evidence that on such tests religious people do gain slightly higher scores than non-religious people, but there is no consistent evidence concerning sudden converts. Scobie (1967) found no evidence that sudden converts were more neurotic than either gradual or unconscious conversion subjects although other investigators (Clark 1928) had found that sudden converts had strong guilt feelings, and Scobie's sample as a whole was more neurotic than the M.M.P.I. student standard-isation group. Although students generally score higher on neuro-ticism tests there is some evidence that younger religious people are more neurotic than their non-religious contemporaries. There-fore, for young people, neuroticism may be another important factor in religious belief and behaviour. It is important to re-member that neuroticism and neurosis are quite distinct, the former being a measure of emotionality or emotional stability and the latter a form of mental illness. There may however be links between the two. For example, religious people seem to have a higher neurosis rate than the non-religious population (Slater 1947).

INTROVERSION

The time available for learning in the sudden conversion experi-ence is severely limited; such circumstances demand rapid condi-tioning. Those individuals who are capable of being conditioned easily and quickly are more able to respond when faced with the evangelistic appeal. Eysenck suggests that it is introverts who condition easily and rapidly and so we might expect to find a higher proportion of introverts among sudden converts. To some extent Scobie confirms this prediction, 44 per cent of his group of 34 converts were classified as introverts, while only 6 per cent were classified as extraverts (χ^2 significant at .01 level). Not only is introversion relevant to religious conversion, but it also seems to be of some general significance in religious belief. Scobie (1967) found that his sample of theological students were more introverted than the estimated norms for the tests and there were more than twice as many extreme introverts in the group than extreme extraverts. If introversion is an important factor in con-version then one would expect the religious sector of the popula-tion to be significantly more introverted than the general popula-tion.

The general implication obtained from this examination of sudden conversion would predict a preponderance of individuals among sudden converts who are either neurotic, or introverted, or both. Some non-neurotics whose emotional response level may have been temporarily elevated by environmental circumstances may also be included.

It is not possible to subject the gradual conversion process to a very detailed examination, and analysis. Investigations are much more difficult because greater individual variations in gradual conversion than in sudden conversion occur, although the same problems seems to be considered by gradual converts as those described by the evangelist to potential sudden converts. The basic difference seems to be one of time, the gradual convert appears to require time in which to consider the implications of belief and commitment. Perhaps there is some resistance to change; the individual may have acquired a number of anti-religious beliefs or attitudes and these need to be overcome before conversion can take place. Once these people have resolved their cognitive dissonance and internalised these beliefs they find it very difficult to modify them at a later date. Eysenck claims that introverts not only condition very quickly but extinguish very slowly. The implication must be that introverts, because they take a long time to extinguish previously held beliefs and attitudes, are more likely to have gradual conversion.

Scobie (1967) did attempt to test this hypothesis. He found 31 per cent of his gradual converts could be classed as extreme introverts, and 16 per cent as extreme extraverts χ^2 significant at .01 level of confidence). The suggestion was made that the result necessitated the extension of the gradual conversion concept to include not only those who are converted in terms of personal religion, that is those who become 'genuinely devout', but also those who are gradually converted and accept the 'extrinsic' value of religion to become 'conventionally religious'. Building on Wilson's (1960) work he found a significant correlation between his measure of extraversion, and measures which Wilson claimed were correlated with the Extrinsic Value Scale. This seems to indicate that extraverted gradual converts have a more conventionally religious set of beliefs. There is a need for additional experimentation to test Scobie's tentative conclusions about gradual conversion, and to explore the sudden conversion process itself.

The unconscious conversion group will probably include a similar proportion of introverts and extraverts. The introverts, because of their rapid conditionability and their slow rate of extinction are more likely to derive religious values and beliefs from their parents and retain them while extraverts, who are slow to condition, will probably respond to the considerable social pressures to conform. If we extend this into the religious sphere, we might find the more extraverted personalities forming the bulk of the conventionally religious. Indeed Scobie found 34 per cent of the unconscious conversion group were extreme introverts and 16 per cent extreme extraverts. All of the introverts had Christian parents and most had very similar beliefs to either their father or mother, or to both parents. A significant correlation between conventional religious values and extraversion was found in this group as well as for the gradual conversion group. The subjects of Scobie's investigations were, of course, students undergoing training for the ministry. It is probable that this sample includes a smaller proportion of the conventionally religious. Such individuals would be unlikely to choose the ministry as a vocation. The small proportion of extraverts in Scobie's complete sample may confirm this conclusion.

If Eysenck's suggestion, that the tender-minded scale represents the projection of introversion onto social attitudes is correct then the religious population should be more tender-minded. Indeed, this has been found the case; religious people, especially the genuinely devout, do score higher in the tender-mindedness scale. It is possible that the reasons for this are two-fold : first, the projection of introversion on social attitudes; and second, the effects of religious beliefs on these same attitudes. Scobie's sample gained a far higher score on tender-mindedness than any of the political groups Eysenck used in his examination of the scale. It is however worth noting that there are a number of religious questions in the tender-mindedness scale, and this could be the principal cause of the finding. Many of the investigations in this area have used student subjects who are generally more introverted than the normal population, in which case the introversion finding for the religious population may be artificially enlarged by the use of a student sample.

POLITICAL ATTITUDES

Political conservatism has already been mentioned in connection with authoritarianism and dogmatism but it is probably an important factor of religious belief in its own right. There are two ways of measuring political attitudes. It can either be determined by the way a person votes or by a questionnaire which is designed to discriminate between people who hold conservative beliefs and those who hold more radical views. In general the results from using political attitude scales seem to indicate that religious people are more conservative than the general population. There seems to be a wide variation between denominations. Roman Catholics appear to be more conservative than Protestants. This may be a result of the problems of producing an adequate random sample, especially if there are similar local variations in political allegiance as there are for ethnocentrism and authoritarianism. The political allegiances of some of the South American priests would certainly not confirm the general conservatism of the Roman Catholic population. The finding that religious people are more conservative than the general population may be an artifact of denominational representation. For a British population, the larger the proportion of Anglicans or Roman Catholics the greater the likelihood that the group will have a higher average score on conservatism than the general population. Scobie (1967) did not find any significant difference in conservatism for his sample in comparison with the general population. This result however may not disprove the suggestion about denominational proportions. Although Anglicans formed the vast majority of his group, the sample has a number of special features. For example all the students were potential church leaders, who may therefore have found it necessary to make rational decisions on certain political issues, unlike the general religious population who may tend to follow the political inclination suggested by their class aspirations.

The voting behaviour of religious people is more complex. The major Protestant denominations in Britain and U.S.A. seem to vote for the more conservative political parties. Roman Catholics, although they have been consistently reported as more conservative in political attitude, seem to favour the radical parties. Such uncharacteristic support may be linked with social class and the status of Roman Catholicism as a minority group in both countries. Social class does have a significant effect on voting behaviour, often conflicting with political attitude scores. American investigations have found that a greater proportion of Protestants than Catholics support the Republican Party. This remains true even when social class is held constant. According to Lazarsfield et al. (1944) three times as many very poor Protestants as opposed to Catholics support the Republican Party. American Protestantism forms of very heterogeneous group and further analysis is necessary before one can determine denominational trends in political voting behaviour.

Eysenck (1954), using a British sample, states that a far larger percentage of religious people vote Conservative compared with the non-religious population. There are also significant denominational differences. Both established Churches in Britain, the Church of England and the Church of Scotland, provide greater Conservative support, whereas the Non-Conformist Churches provide least support for the Conservative Party. Roman Catholics provide the most support for the Labour Party. Scobie (1967) did find that the voting intention of theological students followed the same general pattern as that produced by Eysenck for a religious sample – a large proportion of the sample voted Tory. When the figures were examined in terms of denomination it was found that the Church of England members were the main supporters of the Conservative Party. An analysis of voting intention by social class produced an interesting finding. Comparisons with Eysenck's analysis for the general population are different as he divides his group into five classes while Scobie uses only three classes, but there is some indication after comparison with their non-religious counterparts that the religious middle class gave less support to the Tories and the religious working class gave less support to the Labour Party.

TABLE 6 : SOCIAL CLASS AND VOTING INTENTION

| | | Scobie | | | | Eysenck | |
	Con.	Lab.	Lib.		Con.	Lab.	Lib.
Middle Class N=95	43	25	18	N=2503	60	18	12
Working Class N=61	23	44	21	N=4323	20	60	7

(percentage intending to vote for each Party)

These results do need further investigation, especially as no significant difference between the social classes were found on the political attitude scale. There is however the possibility that religious belief has a significant affect on political voting behaviour. By stressing altruism and the needs of the poor some Protestant Churches may bring about a slight decrease in support for the established bureaucracy. At the same time by its attachment to middle class values it may provide a certain amount of social mobility amongst the working class members, which could result in a support of the Conservative Party.

SUMMARY

Chapter 7 contains an examination of some of the principal factors that have been associated with religious belief and behaviour. The topics discussed were sex, suggestibility, prejudice, authoritarianism, intelligence, neuroticism, introversion, and political attitudes.

8   Sociological Factors in Religious Behaviour

There can be little doubt that a sociological approach to religion provides vital information. In most cases sociological research investigates religion from three avenues: the interaction of religion and society, the religious experience, and the various institutions of religion.

THE INTERACTION OF RELIGION AND SOCIETY

The first avenue is concerned with the influence society has had on religion and also the influence of religion on society. It brings to the fore one particular sociological viewpoint known as 'functional theory' in which all institutions are seen to interact and modify one another to form the dynamic unity we refer to as the social system, or, perhaps less accurately, as society. Such considerations as these lead us to enquire why men need religious belief. In other words, it is an attempt to determine the function and purpose of religion for society. In this area two names stand out, those of Weber and Durkheim. Weber's contribution was twofold. First he drew attention (Weber 1905) to the influence of Protestantism on the development of capitalism, and argued that the ethical concepts (especially those concerned with money) propounded by Protestants were significant in the development of a capitalist society. Secondly, he maintained that religion was an attempt to answer the universal problem of meaning in the lives of individuals; and in its answer, religion determines and influences a large area of activity and behaviour in the life of an adherent.

Durkheim (1897) argued that religion was an attempt to embody all the traditions and demands of society into an ordered acceptable whole. God was a personal expression of society. Thus man's religion as preserving society. It is one of the most important methods standards of his society and culture. In this way Durkheim saw religion as preserving society It is one of the most important methods of preventing the collapse of society and ensuring the commitment of each individual to the well-established and widely-accepted standards.

Social Class

Not only has society been influenced and modified by religion, but society modifies and affects religion. That is perhaps seen best in the investigations of religious belief and behaviour in the different social classes or racial groups. The characteristics of the religious beliefs in the various groups seem to be significantly different.

In Britain most measures indicate that the upper and middle class are most active in religion and the working class are least active. An examination of religious beliefs does not produce quite the same pattern. There is a tendency for the working class to be more favourably inclined to the Church and to accept more of its religious concepts than might be expected, given the level of religious participation. On some measures working class scores are similar to, or even above, those of the upper class. The two scales used in the most recent survey (I.T.A. 1970), religiosity, and endorsement of traditional Christian beliefs confirm this finding (see table 5, p. 110). It can be seen that the upper and upper middle class show the highest percentage of individuals in the higher grades of the religiosity scale, and yet the same group has the lowest proportion of people who are certain there is a God. The skilled working class have the same proportion for religiosity and belief in God; they seem to be the least religious over-all. The semi-skilled and very poor categories also have the same proportions on both scales but as a group they are slightly more religious. The lower middle class present the opposite pattern to the upper and upper middle class. This group shows by far the highest percentage of people who are certain there is a God but they have the next lowest percentage on the religiosity scale.

It is interesting to note that in the U.S.A. the religious activity/social class structure is a little different. Here, the middle class are most active. The possibility now emerges in the light of these findings that the middle class are the most active group in both countries, but that in Britain the middle class is in some way alienated from the Church so that, although its belief in God is unaffected, it does not play the same part in church activities as its American counterpart. Further evidence is necessary, however, before any definite conclusions can be drawn.

There may be purely practical reasons for the class differences in religious participation. It is possible that the middle class have more time available for religious activities. The working class spend

a larger proportion of their time at their work, especially on over-
time. The business and professional classes may be at their place of
work for a shorter time, but their job can demand additional time
and effort outside the office. The middle or lower working class
however, will usually hold the traditional 9.00 a.m. to 5.00 p.m.
job, and are more likely to have fewer demands on their time
outside working hours. This explanation seems to be quite adequate for the American situation but the British picture is more
complex. The structure of the upper class in Britain may be quite
different to the U.S.A. Britain has a traditional élite derived from
the landed gentry whose vocational demands might be low. Such
a group might account for the higher rate of religious activity by
the upper and upper middle classes in Britain. There is still the
problem of the restricted activity of the lower middle class. It is
possible that in British society this is now one of the most economic-
ally-deprived groups. While the wages of the working class have
been rising, those of the clerical workers who form the bulk of the
lower middle class have not kept pace. It could mean that the group
is now under greater pressure than the working class to supplement
their income with part-time jobs, which leave less time for attendance at church and other religious functions.

Some investigators have contended that class is an important factor
in determining the character of religious attitudes. Goode (1966) for
example suggests that church-linked activities have become 'secular-
ised' for the middle class religious person; while for the religious working class person church activities have retained greater religious
significance. Estus and Overington (1970) duplicated Goode's work
on a larger sample and were unable to agree with his findings. They
maintain that his results can be attributed to his insistence on
making a sacred/secular division. Instead of making such a division
they used a measure of integration which is a variable ' containing
all elements in a members relationship to a congregation '. They
maintain that social class and church participation is a valid
approach to the sociology of religion. They also state that most
churches are organised around middle class values and styles, and
that those who participate have realised, or aspirant, middle class
values. In other words, middle class members have the opportunity
in church activities to act out their realised middle class values;
whole working class individuals should be seen as people who aspire
to the middle class and their church activity provides ' " on the
job training " in that life-style, in spite of their actual lower class
status ', Goode (1970) is quick to retaliate, not in criticism of their
research work but of their interpretation. He points out that many

researchers have found a positive relation between social class and church attendance, but a negative one between social class and religious devotion. It is this apparent contradiction between these authors which necessitates research. No doubt the controversy will continue, but the extent of the significance claimed for social class by Estus and Overington does need considerably more empirical evidence.

The importance of social class seems to apply even to the less institutionalised religious groups. Nelson et al. (1972) investigated the reasons why individuals had joined the Spiritualist National Union. They found that followers listed a number of causes, from the possession of psychic gifts, to dissatisfaction with existing Christian denominations. Members however tended to come from the middle class and to be occupationally mobile. Again, in this situation there seems to be a marked absence of working class participation.

Another explanation for the difference in religious activity between the classes may be directly related to the outreach of the Church itself. The major Protestant denominations seem to be better geared to contacting the upper and middle classes and show a singular ineptitude in approaching the working class (especially in Britain). The Roman Catholic Church with its greater stress on outward observance seems better able to retain the allegiance of the working class. Another point to bear in mind in this situation is the contention that the Protestant ethic facilitates upward social mobility. Most surveys determine social class and religious activity at the same moment in time. It could be anticipated therefore, that social mobility produced by religious belief would result in a lower proportional representation of the working class. There are many equally plausible explanations for the affects of social class on religious belief and behaviour and additional research is required before the position can be clarified.

Achievement Motivation and Career Choice

McClelland (1961) in his work on achievement levels examined Weber's hypothesis linking Protestantism and capitalism. He compared the achievement scores of Catholics and Protestants. In most cases there is a slight but significant difference favouring the Protestants. Usually variations in social class made useful comparisons almost impossible. He does, however, cite one instance where comparisons can be made : two Mexican villages, one Protestant, one folk-Catholic, are examined and he finds evidence of greater achievement motivation for the Protestants. This may

E

be due to the need for Protestants to read the Bible. which in turn produces a higher literacy rate in the Protestant village. However, there is need for further research work in this area.

Another important associated problem, is the effect of religious belief in career selection. Greeley (1963) examined the influence of the Protestant ethic and compared the career choice and orientation of Protestants and Catholics. Previous work had indicated that Catholics tend to have a bias against the selection of science as a career subject. He was unable to find any significant differences between Protestants and Catholics, except that a greater number of Catholics chose business as a career and preferred to work in large corporations. He suggested that the failure to find significant differences might be caused by the variations in the ethnic compositions of his group in comparison with that of Lenski (1960) and others. He maintains that the ethnic factor is an important one in American culture. Greeley (1969) managed to re-examine many of these students seven years later and was able to substantially confirm his initial findings.

In contrast to Greeley's results, Jackson et al. (1970) maintain that Protestants are more likely to enter professional and business occupations than Catholics, who in turn are more likely to enter white-collar occupations than Protestants. These comparisons are made between individuals of the same occupational origin. They also found that Protestants are 'more often sharply upward mobile' and Catholics 'more often sharply downward mobile'. All these differences they maintain persist even when controls for race, region of origin, age, generation, and size of community of origin, are controlled. It would seem obvious from these conflicting results that additional research is urgently needed in order to try and clarify the situation.

Another recent investigation which may throw some indirect light on the problem is that of Rhodes and Nam (1970). They found that the extent to which an individual plans for a college education is dependent on the religion of the mother and the religious composition of the school. This holds true even when a number of items are controlled, such as individual intelligence, family income, mother's educational attainment, and occupation of the head of the household. They conclude that these results support the contention that some religious denominations stress the value and thereby encourage an individual's desire for higher education. They tend to support Jackson et al. (1970) by their suggestion that Protestants have higher occupational achievement. The conflict between their results and those of Greeley may be due to the composition of the Protestant group. Some Protestant denominations stress the value of higher education far more than others.

Sex and Marriage

The influence of religious belief on marriage, sexual attitudes and family life provide another important sociological approach to religion. For example, Kitay (1947) found that people who had favourable attitudes towards religion tended to come from homes with a more religious and harmonious background. In addition such people were more conservative in politics and economics and had fewer sexual difficulties than other individuals who held unfavourable attitudes to religion.

In a study of the parents of college students Fisher (1948) was able to ascertain, using the Allport-Vernon-Lindzey Study of Values, that similarity of religious values was more important than similarity of any other of the measured values for the success of a marriage. Landis (1949) was able to study inter-faith marriages by using a large sample of college students and enquiring about the religious beliefs of the parents. He found that where parents held initially different religious affiliations, one partner tended to change. If this modification in affiliation did occur, there was less likelihood of divorce in comparison with parents who maintained their separate religious beliefs. Couples who agreed about religion were more likely to have very happy marriages than those who disagreed. The percentages he gives are quite striking, 65 per cent compared with 9 per cent for those who do not agree about religion. Burchinal (1957) pointed out, however, that matters of finance and how to spend time together were more important to marital adjustment than agreement on religion, but when both husband and wife attend church regularly they gain higher scores on scales of marital satisfaction than couples who attend church irregularly, or not at all.

Wallin (1957) and Wallin and Clark (1964) investigated the relationship between sexual enjoyment and marital satisfaction. They found that women with a high score on religiosity still gained general marital satisfaction, even though they had some lack of sexual gratification. This finding did not apply to the men in the sample. Cavan (1972) has examined the attitude of Jewish college students to inter-religion marriages. There was quite a difference in attitude between Conservative and Reform Jews, the conservatives insisting on endogamy, while a large proportion of the Reform group were in favour of marriage inside, or outside the Jewish race. Both groups, however, were slightly more in favour of marriage to Protestants than to Catholics. Prince (1972) looked at the problem of Protestant/Catholic intermarriage. There was a whole range of cultural differences, as well as differences in religious belief which would place considerable strain on marriages of this kind.

It would seem that where religion forms an integral part of the development of attitudes and life-styles, then interfaith marriages face considerable difficulties. The couple not only have differences in religious belief, but their attitudes on numerous secular items are profoundly different.

RELIGIOUS EXPERIENCE

The second area of research is the most difficult to compartment-alise. Both psychology and sociology are concerned with the same phenomena and use similar methods and techniques. There is certainly interaction between religious experience and social/cultural forces. For example, certain more extreme denominations and sects demand a sudden conversion experience as a prerequisite for membership. There is some evidence that the incidence of sudden conversion is higher in such groups and, of course, the experience opens up a wider field of social contacts within the group. This same argument also applies to the significance of glossolalia in a number of Pentecostal groups. These problems have already been considered within a psychological framework and no further comment seems necessary.

INSTITUTIONS OF RELIGION

The third research area suggested, deals with the institutionalisation of religion : how the particular belief patterns emerge and how the organisation develops.

Sects

This approach is probably best illustrated by investigations of the development of sects. Boisen (1955) noted that sects (at least those in America) seem to develop initially among the socially deprived. A fundamental part of their belief system is the Protestant ethic regarding the use of money. Adherents begin to live according to the rule of stewardship : they begin to save money and become more prosperous. At this point Boisen maintains that the members begin to look for a professional minister with a middle class outlook and education; from then on the sect begins to lose its initial features and take on the character of a denomination. With this development, internal conflict might occur and those individuals who have been unable or unwilling to climb the social status ladder tend to rebel and try to start another sect. In this way the process is perpetuated.

The sects and other religious minority groups have also been investigated by Yinger (1957). He suggested that there were three broad types :

(1) Those who passively accept their underprivileged status and emphasise religious values only.

(2) Those who withdraw from society, criticise it but do not attack it.

(3) Those who are vigorous in their attack on society, condemning it on religious grounds.

These two authors illustrate the value of examining the institutionalisation of religion. They emphasise once again the extent of the interaction between religion and society.

Church Activity and Organisation
There have been investigations of religious institutions from other points of view. Perhaps the most interesting deals with the activity and organisation of the institution.

It has often been shown that religious activity in rural areas is much higher than in large towns and cities. In Britain the attendance figures indicate that 17 per cent of the population of small towns attend church but only 12 per cent of those living in large cities go to church each week. In France the difference is even greater, 60 per cent of the rural population as opposed to 25 per cent of the urban poulation are regular attenders at Mass. These figures however say nothing of the quality of religious observance in urban and rural areas. Carlos (1970) investigated in detail the effect of distance from the centre of a city or metropolitan area on religious attendance. His subjects were the Catholic population of Montreal. He had two measures of religious activity, Mass attendance and attendance at Communion. The former he maintains is a cultic measure relating to what Argyle refers to as conventional religion, the latter being a measure of genuine devotion, or personal religion. His findings indicate that in the suburbs there is a higher rate of attendance, but this is on the nominal measure, Mass attendance. There is no corresponding increase in personal devotion; in fact the measures indicate that larger proportions of the population in the centre of conurbations engage in personal religious practices.

An investigation of the claimed theological position of a church in terms of a fundamentalist/modernist continuum was undertaken by Moberg (1970). He found that such a dimension has significant correlations with the composition and character of a church. For example, the more conservative a church the less paid staff there is; the more Sunday School classes in relation to the size of the congregation, the higher the church attendance, and the higher the per capita budget. On the other hand the more liberal a church is, the larger its membership, and the greater likelihood it has declined in size and is racially inclusive. These findings are very interesting because they seem to tie in with some of the findings associated with the personality characteristics of the individuals who make up the respective churches.

There has been some attempt to compare the beliefs held by the institution (e.g. the denomination), the individual and the church congregations. For example, Davidson (1972) compared patterns of religious belief at denominational and congregational levels. He examined homogeneity (one belief dominating all others) and heterogeneity (several belief patterns) of religious beliefs. The findings indicated that heterogeneity seemed to apply at the denominational level. Among the four congregations studied only one demonstrated homogeneity of religious beliefs. The subjects were Baptists and Methodists, and there would perhaps be greater variation if other denominations were considered. Spaulding (1972) compared the beliefs of individuals and the official formulation of their denomination. He found considerable variation and suggested that investigations of this kind would help ministers decide on areas of doctrine presenting difficulties to their congregation.

Another area of interest is the affect of changes in society on the role played by various members of an institution. Perhaps it is the clergy of established Churches who have been under most pressure. This is particularly true of the Church of England. The parish priest was once a leading authority, often one of the few learned men in the community. Now he is only one of many, and often a large number of his congregation are better educated than he is, added to which there are professional social workers who cover many of its 'charitable' acts. He therefore faces a role crisis. What should he be doing in the community in which he lives and for the congregation he serves (see Bocock 1970)?

Sociologists are also concerned in collecting information about the size and distribution of various institutions. There are, of course, regular surveys and censuses which indicate the number of members of a particular denomination, or religious group. Occasionally more detailed studies give some idea of the nature of beliefs that are held in a community and what effect this might have in terms of organisation. In general statistics of this kind are linked to other variables, such as ethnic background, class, marital status, sex, geographical area, etc.

SUMMARY

In this chapter an attempt has been made to examine the sociological factors associated with religious behaviour. The topics covered were social class, achievement motivation and career choice, sex and marriage, sects, church activity and organisation.

Attitude Change in Religious Behaviour

It is necessary to consider attitude development in order to be able to examine changes in attitude. Most individual attitudes are formed during childhood and adolescence; they are usually acquired from parents, society, or the peer group. Parents are the principal influence in attitude formation, for they pass on many of the mores of society, as well as their own individual attitudes. The significant influence of parents can be illustrated by voting behaviour. Where both parents agree on party preference more than 80 per cent of the children examined voted for the same party as their parents (Butler and Stokes 1969). There is a decline as the children move away from parental influence but it still seems to remain at about the 70 per cent level.

There may be differences in the way parents and siblings hold their beliefs even when they are identical in content. If the child internalises the beliefs, then they become a source of internal motivation, producing what has been referred to in the religious sphere as the 'genuinely devout', or the 'intrinsically motivated'. Alternatively, the child may see the value of behaving in a way acceptable to the parents, conforming on purely practical grounds, but he may not accept the inner motive for such beliefs and behaviour, in which case he could be termed a conventionally religious person, extrinsically motivated. A third possibility is the child who accepts the beliefs and values of the parents, while under their influence. However, as soon as this influence diminishes, usually when he no longer lives with the parents, he rejects the beliefs at the intrinsic and extrinsic level. This process seems adequate to describe the development of religious attitudes and can be applied to other areas of behaviour. The final outcome in terms of the attitudes held by the individual is, of course, related to the beliefs of the parents. For example, the child can only develop intrinsic religious attitudes if (1) the parents are intrinsically motivated, (2) he correctly perceives their intrinsic religious attitudes, and (3) he internalises the beliefs. These three factors are vital for the development of the genuinely devout. If the parents have conflicting beliefs, then additional influences become important, such as which parent exercises most influence in the area of religious belief. The extent of the child's identification with either, or with both parents, must be taken into account as this will have a bearing on the internalisation process.

Not only do parents pass on some of society's standards to their children, but often parents use some of society's institutions to facilitate beliefs and attitudes that they wish their children to develop. They may also exercise some control of the peer group of the child, of which perhaps a good example is the selection of a public or boarding school or the fact that many Christians may send their children to Sunday School. Although there are a number of individual variations in the development of religious attitudes it would seem that belief (or unbelief) is mediated through the parents (or parent substitutes), often assisted by society and the peer group. Occasionally the three influences may be at variance with one another, and then the individual has to resolve the conflict. Adolescence seems to be the time when such conflict is likely to occur and this could be why so many religious conversions take place during this period. Adolescence is the period during which decisions affecting many areas of life, including religious belief, are taken.

As a consequence of the processes described above a person may be genuinely devout, conventionally religious, non-religious, anti-religious, or he may oscillate from one attitude to another. Given the religious attitude of the individual the next problem is whether it is amenable to change. Attitudes are generally quite resistant to change; the processes of selection and social reinforcement usually prevent the modification of attitudes. People usually selectively perceive material which is consistent with their existing attitudes, e.g. socialists select material for active consideration which is generally consistent with their socialist ideology. People join groups holding similar opinions to their own and in this way gain social support for their own beliefs. There are, however, processes which can change attitudes. These may be grouped into three categories :

(1) rational or intellectual persuasion,
(2) emotional persuasion,
(3) physiological persuasion.

Rational persuasion deals with the process of changing attitudes by the presentation of information. If information is presented in an unbiased way it is usually referred to as education. Propaganda is the term used when material is proffered favourable to one side to the exclusion or misrepresentation of material supporting the opposite point of view. If the information is new to the individual its assimilation can be instrumental in beginning the process of attitude change. Alternatively it may be the way old material is presented, for example forcibly or logically, which the person finds convincing.

Emotional persuasion, as the name suggests, is an attempt to change attitudes by emotional means. Such attempts may be presented in a pseudo-rational way; arguing for the return of the death penalty on the basis of how a person would feel if his own daughter was raped and murdered. The more usual alternative is persuasion by a good orator within a highly emotional setting, such as the mass meetings of Billy Graham crusades or the Nuremburg Rallies of Hitler.

Physiological persuasion or brain washing is the process employed by interrogators to bring about physical, emotional, and mental exhaustion. Subjects in this state seem more ready either to divulge secret information, or adopt, perhaps only temporarily, beliefs and attitudes suggested by their interrogators. Such processes were first investigated and described by Pavlov and applied to the interpretation of religious conversion by Sargant (see chapter 6).

In the first part of this chapter the effects of education and training on religious belief are examined. The previous paragraphs have indicated the importance such effects can have on the development of belief and the change of attitudes by rational persuasion. The rest of the chapter considers religious propagation, and the work of the teacher, preacher and evangelist as agents in the process. Their differential influence on the three types of conversion experience and techniques they might adopt to improve the effectiveness of their efforts are also considered. Anti-religious attitudes can also be disseminated but with the exception of the Humanist Society there seems little organised effort to promote such beliefs.

THE EFFECTS OF EDUCATION AND TRAINING ON RELIGIOUS BELIEF

The increasing proportion of national resources devoted to education gives ample proof of the influence it has on every part of our lives. In this section we consider the way a person's beliefs develop or change as a consequence of his educational experiences. This can be quite a difficult assignment. An alternative is to compare matched groups at different stages within the educational process. Perhaps one of the earliest investigators to do this was Betts (1929). He compared the beliefs of 700 ministers and theological students and found that the students had more liberal ideas and did not accept many of the traditional beliefs. This may merely indicate the general development of more liberal beliefs in American Protestantism during the period. However, work by Shand (1968) indicates that this is more than just the operation of new theological ideas reaching and influencing the students before the ministers. He found in his twenty-year follow-up study of the religious beliefs of 114 Amherst College students, that while belief systems were relatively permanent on a number of variables there were some changes toward greater belief, especially the literal acceptance of the Biblical account of the life, crucifixion, and resurrection of Christ.

Woodward (1932) was directly interested in the relationship between present beliefs and past religious training and influence. He found significant correlation between the beliefs of adults and their rating of parental religious influence. Quite often secular education can have an effect on religious beliefs. This fact emerged from Nathan's (1932) investigation. Sixty per cent of the Jewish students he examined admitted that they experienced conflict or doubt over their traditional religious ideas and the scientific and secular information they were learning. It is possible that the inferior status of women within orthodox Judaism (but not in Western society), is responsible for another of his findings, that there are fewer Jewish women with orthodox beliefs among large samples of students.

Leuba (1934), investigating the beliefs of eminent scientists, found considerable differences in belief between scientists belonging to the various fields of knowledge. A greater proportion of scientists concerned with inanimate objects (such as physicists) believe in God and immortality than scientists investigating human behaviour (psychologists).

It is possible that the social pressure which exists in most educational institutions is mainly responsible for changes in religious belief. Certain investigators have indicated that religious belief is significantly influenced by social pressure. Burtt and Falkenburg (1941) gave a religious attitude scale to 213 church members. A third of the subjects were later told the majority opinion, a third the views of a group of clergymen, and the remainder were told nothing at all and constituted the control group. The test was then re-administered and it was found that subjects tended to change their opinions significantly in the direction of the majority opinion, or the expert opinion of the clergymen in comparison with the control group subjects. Brown and Pallant (1962) conducted a similar experiment, but this time the social pressure was provided for a group of Methodist adolescents by a report of beliefs purported to be held by a prominent Methodist minister, and another set of beliefs were said to be those of a Roman Catholic priest. There was a significant trend by the adolescents to modify their beliefs in the direction of those held by the Methodist minister and a tendency to move away from those held by the priest.

A number of studies have investigated changes in religious belief and attitude by students during their years of study. Arsenian (1943) using the Allport and Vernon Study of Values questionnaire found that there were significant changes in the value pattern of student subjects during their four year study period. The changes seem to have been dependent on the curricular and extra-curricular activities of the student. He found evidence of much religious re-adjustment, religious beliefs tending to become more liberal in outlook and orientation. A British university student sample has been similarly investigated. Poppleton and Pilkington (1963) produced their own Religious Attitude Scale and found that there was a decline in religious belief in Arts and Pure Science students during their first year of study. This decline is reversed for Art students later in their course but not for Science students.

Allport, Gillespie and Young (1948) were interested in the religious beliefs of students and especially the effect war service had on such beliefs. Their subjects were studying at Harvard (male) and Radcliffe (female). The Harvard sample was divided into those who had fought during World War II and those who had not. The Radcliffe group was not split, as only one subject had fought during the war. Their general findings indicated that 70 per cent of the students felt some religious orientation was necessary for a full life. A majority of the students observed some traditional religious practice (such as prayer) but only 25 per cent were orthodox in their beliefs. In general it appeared that religious belief played a significant part in the life of most of the students, but such beliefs were of a radical nature. A similar picture seems to apply to those Harvard students who had experienced war service. They appear to have less attachment to orthodox and traditional religious practices and beliefs but a greater interest in religion and the problems religion seeks to solve in comparison with students without war service.

This process away from orthodoxy towards a more radical and social religious outlook seems to have continued over the years. A recent survey of Harvard and Radcliffe students using the same method as Allport et al. was conducted by Eddy (1968). He found that beliefs had become more liberal and there had been a decline in church attendance from 25 per cent to 20 per cent for men and from 49 per cent to 20 per cent for women. He also found an increase in the directing of religious beliefs into social problem areas rather than into orthodox religious behaviour. He sounds a note of caution in this useful comparative study, namely possible changes in selection criterion between the years 1946–1966. Another longitudinal study was conducted by Bender (1958) who was able to re-examine a number of individuals who had previously been tested and interviewed in 1940 as Dartmouth College students. The Allport-Vernon Study of Values Test indicates a significant increase in religious interest over the years between test and re-test. This finding together with a decrease in economic interest are the only significant changes in the test. The suggestion that the changes in scores are a function of changes in society and not changes in personal maturity were confirmed by a comparison of this group with a group of students attending the college at the time. It was found that test scores completed by both former and present students in 1956 were remarkably similar; there were no significant differences. It would seem from this that the influence of society affects religious interest more than individual development.

If social pressure was the only factor operating then the subject studied by the individual should have little influence on religious belief. This is not the case, investigations indicate that the subject of study is very important.

Teachers in the physical and social sciences were investigated by Rogers (1966). In general the subjects did not accept the beliefs of the strict believer, the general public, formal Christianity, or Judaism. Where changes in religious belief had taken place 50 per cent of the subjects reported that these occurred during their time at college. If the change was away from religious belief then scientific method and theory were of prime importance, but if it was towards greater religious belief then scientific principles were not seemingly important in the change. In general the research findings indicate that the study of science leads to a continuous decline in religious belief, whereas for arts and perhaps social science subjects there is a slight reversal of the decline in the final year of study. These slight differences may be related to the basic philosophy underlying the subject. The truth, or otherwise, of religious concepts are outside the scope of scientific investigation. They are not amenable to empirical study and analysis and since the training that scientists receive encourages them to doubt and criticise all claims which have not been scientifically verified, this scepticism will probably increase with training and experience. The Arts student, and to a lesser extent the Social Science student gains experience of many different philosophical and religious ideas which may encourage him to re-examine some of his original decisions about religious concepts and generally to be more open to non-scientific material. These assumptions are to some extent supported by the finding that scientists have a greater intolerance of ambiguity than non-scientists.

The decline in religious belief during attendance at college or university may not be the direct result of the educational process. It is necessary to see this decline against the background of the general decline with age during the period eighteen to thirty years. It is possible that the effects of greater concern with family and work during the period and the increased scepticism which might be encouraged by the educational process may be additive and produce the surprising drop in religious activity during college or university education.

Attendance at Sunday School has been seen as an important contributing factor to the development and maintenance of religious belief. But again it is difficult to determine whether the effect is due to the education received at Sunday School, or to having religious parents who insist on sending their children to Sunday School. In connection with this problem Woodward (1932) found a higher correlation between Sunday School attendance, and subsequent conservatism in religious beliefs, than he found between attendance and the religious activity of parents. In Britain the situation may be somewhat different, children may be sent to Sunday School even when their parents do not attend church themselves, or do not have any religious beliefs. This may result from a desire for the child to have some religious teaching; or from a more mercenary attitude which merely makes use of the child-minding facilities provided each Sunday by the church. The rapid decline in Sunday School membership may be the result of these parents no longer sending their children to Sunday School but preferring to take them for a drive in the country.

Both Clark (1928) and Woodward (1932) claimed that subjects who had attended Sunday School were less likely to have a sudden conversion experience. Scobie (1967) was unable to confirm this finding when comparing the three conversion types. He argued that if sudden converts had only attended Sunday School after their conversion, they will obviously have attended for fewer years than those who went throughout their childhood. No significant differences were found between the means of the three groups. He suggests that a change in the character of Sunday School teaching over the years may be responsible for the conflicting results. Perhaps the emphasis in modern Sunday Schools is more on the stories of the Bible and social action rather than the doctrines of sin and salvation and this teaching is not so relevant to the sudden conversion process.

The other point that needs to be considered is the possibility that training and education have a differential influence on the three conversion types. There is little information on this problem, except for that provided by Scobie (1967). He tried to determine the affect of theological training on religious belief by calculating the correlation between measures of religious conservatism and number of years at theological college. The results indicate that the type of training appears to influence the score on religious conservatism. Students who had been attending a conservative college for a number of years tended to be more conservative than those who had recently joined the college. Where the teaching was of a more liberal kind the established students tended to be more liberal than those who were new to the college. In addition there was a significant difference between conversion types and the amount of change that occurred as a result of training. Sudden converts do not seem to be influenced to any extent by training, whereas the gradual and, to a lesser degree, the unconscious conversion group become more liberal in religious belief. There is an apparent inconsistency in Scobie's findings. If sudden converts are unaffected by training and the gradual and unconscious types become more liberal, how do students at a conservative college become more conservative? The answer appears to lie in the composition of the groups. Seventy three per cent of the sudden converts attended the conservative college, while only 29 per cent of the gradual and 18 per cent of the unconscious conversion group attended the college. If we assume that the change in religious attitudes for sudden converts is minimal then any change must be the result of the gradual and unconscious conversion types at that college becoming more conservative. This movement would be hidden in the overall correlation coefficient because of the relatively small numbers of these groups at the college. It implies, of course, that the gradual and unconscious conversion types at the liberal colleges become more liberal than the statistics would seem to indicate. The general conclusion that can be made is that whereas the gradual and unconscious conversion types are influenced by the kind of training they receive, the sudden converts seems to be only mildly affected by training. The complaint levelled at many funda-

mentalists and literalists (who will probably be mainly sudden converts) that they are not susceptible to rational argument, may
provide additional evidence for the conclusion drawn here.

Religious Propagation

The investigations of Sunday school and theological college training calls for a more detailed examination of religious education
in all its many forms. Probably the best way to do this is to
examine the problem from the point of view of the teacher, the
preacher, and the evangelist.

One important point needs clarification before we begin, and it
concerns the distinction between religious knowledge and religious
commitment, between information about, and involvement in,
religion or Christianity. Many people in Britain know and are
even taught the facts of the Christian faith but relatively few are
personally committed to it. At this point we recall the different
meanings of belief noted by Spinks (1960), 'knowledge about'
is not equivalent to 'belief in' a given subject. In some cases
supposed knowledge may deter a person from religious commitment. The acquisition of religious information may be mistakenly
understood by some people as the quintessence of the Christian
faith. It is possible that compulsory religious education in British
schools has significantly contributed to the decline in church
attendance, so having the opposite effect to the one intended. The
situation in America, where there is no compulsory religious
education, could be interpreted as confirming this idea. There is
greater religious participation, but less religious knowledge (Rosten 1955) in the U.S.A. So those who seek to maintain Christianity
by insisting on religious education in schools are perhaps in-
advertently helping to undermine it.

There are then two aspects of religious belief, namely information
and commitment. If the principle concern is conveying information
about religion or Christianity, then religion can be treated in the
same way as any other academic subject. However, if an attempt
is being made to evoke commitment and involvement in religion,
then a different approach may be necessary. Religion, in this sense,
forms one of the principal subjects in quite another category,
a category in which participants are not only required 'to know'
but 'to do or behave' and perhaps at a still deeper level 'to be',
whatever the beliefs demand. All religious, ethical, and moral
systems and perhaps to a lesser extent the cultural and traditional
mores of the society to which the individual belongs, are in this
category. The religious propagation process we are now discussing

is no longer simply educational but is concerned with persuasion, indoctrination, and attitude change. It is perhaps for this reason that fundamentalist evangelism arouses so much antagonism, for its advocates blatantly attempt to persuade rather than educate those who attend their meetings. It is very difficult to present religious or moral principles in order to arouse commitment and involvement. The increase in crime and violence in our society would indicate that in this area of education and socialisation, Western civilisation is relatively inept.

Religious education, then, may have a dual purpose, to provide knowledge and induce commitment. Probably the ideal presentation is to stress both aspects but often only one is emphasised to the exclusion of the other. We have already discussed the general character of compulsory religious education in Britain and the possible detrimental effect it may have on religious activity. It is also possible that the large number of sudden converts who lose their faith, do so because the evangelistic address concentrates on religious commitment, and tends to minimise the importance of information. The propagation of religious belief is a complex procedure and all those involved in religious education, not only teachers but also preachers and evangelists need to consider the implications of the research investigations in the psychology of religion.

The Teacher

Teaching is a broad term, including not only the work of the professional but also the parents' efforts to educate their children, especially during the pre-school years. There are many other people who play some part in religious education : ministers, Sunday School teachers, and youth club leaders – all contribute in the propagation of the Christian faith.

Professional teachers of religion are normally restricted to some extent by having to complete a stipulated syllabus. It usually means that they have to concentrate on teaching religious information at a purely descriptive level and maintain a completely neutral attitude to the material discussed. There may be, however, occasions when the teacher's presentation of material produces a more profound response than the mere absorption of information. The teacher's attitudes or interest in his field of study may stimulate the student to a similar degree of involvement. In addition, during the early years of schooling, there is much more exploration and less formal instruction and class organisation, and this could provide an atmosphere favourable to the development of religious commitment.

The methods a teacher uses to evoke religious or moral commitment are not vigorously applied; very often they derive from the unconscious attitudes and the unintentional impressions the teacher may give. In this sense religious commitment is not taught and there is no educational technique employed in order to produce Christians who are deeply involved in their religion. Nevertheless, there are principles which when applied seem to encourage children to adopt similar attitudes and to become involved in the same things as their parents or teachers. Some of the teaching methods employed by Chinese Communist teachers, for example ritual denouncements of imperialism and ritual praise for Chairman Mao, are obviously intended to produce committed Maoists. Western culture would be unwiling to accept such techniques as it prefers the method of rational persuasion rather than indoctrination. There is very little scientific evidence that such techniques do result in genuine commitment; they are, perhaps, more likely to produce passive acceptance. It is possible that they only provide information, and do not result in active participation.

What principles can be used so that teachers can directly influence the religious participation of their pupils? It is at this point that the problem becomes even more complex. It is obvious that the extent of a teacher's influence and the methods which prove most effective are partly deteremined by the personality of the child. The more authoritarian a child, the greater the likelihood that he will be influenced by the teacher's status as a person of authority rather than by the rational arguments the teacher may expound. But authoritarianism seems to be a direct result of early childhood training, the parent demanding obedience on the basis of his parental status. So the system seems self-perpetuating. The initial exercise of status authority by the parent over the child makes him more susceptible to similar authority on subsequent occasions. If, however, the teacher loses status or esteem in the eyes of the child then all the attitudes and interests derived from that person are likely to be jettisoned. Therefore such a system is a very risky method of encouraging religious commitment. The rebellion of the adolescent against the morals and standards of society may be a consequence of the declining status of the parents. As the child grows older, so the parents seem to lose many of their god-like qualities. If status authority has been the main teaching method in the home, then the decline in status may result in the denouncement of all parental attitudes, including any religious commitment.

The child who is not particularly authoritarian presents a different problem. Such children have normally received explanations and justifications for the questions they have asked and the action they have been expected to perform. These methods also need to be applied to the moral and religious area of development. The child needs to be told not only how things work but also why certain actions are desirable or necessary. This will involve complex arguments about the necessity of a moral and religious way of life.

We have distinguished between authoritarian and non-authoritarian children, but such a distinction is an oversimplification. Investigators in the area of moral development (Kay 1968) have identified a number of stages in which different attitudes predominate. Four major stages seem to occur; prudential, authoritarian, social, and personal, in that order, although moral development may be arrested at any one stage. Progression to a later stage does not necessarily preclude the occurrence of attitudes more appropriate to an earlier level. Thus at certain stages of mental growth, authoritative pronouncements may be the most appropriate method of teaching moral and religious commitment. Later in their development the explanations and justifications of religious action become far more desirable. It is extremely important that the teacher is aware of the stage of development of each pupil and which kind of training is appropriate.

Kay emphasises the teacher's ability to modify and change attitudes. He also discusses the three main areas, already mentioned, where attitude change can be facilitated : the status or credibility of the communicator, in this case the teacher, the way the information is communicated, and the characteristics and personality of the individuals who are listening. The opinion and example provided by the high status teacher is more likely to be followed and adopted than that of one who has lost credibility and holds little status. Thus the example and attitude of certain teachers is extremely important for the development of religious commitment. The ways in which a teacher attains high status in the eyes of his class are very varied. They usually depend on the enthusiasm the teacher expresses for his subject and a genuine interest in the individuals he teaches.

Any person who attempts to change other people's attitudes usually tries to substantiate his arguments by providing detailed explanations, and he also stresses the advantages of holding his attitude and the disadvantages or dangers of not accepting his particular opinions. Professional teachers, as we have already noted, are principally concerned with imparting information and rarely seek to change attitudes. On the occasions that they do express their own opinions they probably prefer to use substantive arguments to justify their attitudes rather than stressing the positive and negative values of accepting their position. Other religious educators especially evangelists, seems to use all three methods in their attempts to change attitudes and induce religious commitment.

The three conversion types seem to indicate the principal ways in which people become religious. One would anticipate that religious education would have a differential affect on potential converts, either contributing to the development of the three types of conversion, or helping to maintain their separate identity, or probably doing both.

The description of the unconscious conversion type would indicate a preponderance of positive influences on religious development. They have probably received authoritative religious guidance from their parents and also adequate explanation and justification for religious belief from most of the high status figures in their lives. In other words, the teacher should be able, given the necessary freedom of action, to meet the developing needs of the child which are required to produce moral and religious maturity. The development of religious commitment in such an individual seems to be the direct result of what may be called a teaching ministry.

The unconscious conversion process seems to be a quite natural development. The question one needs to ask is why it does not develop in every person and why in some cases a gradual or sudden conversion is necessary to produce religious commitment? It would appear that people who do not have an unconscious conversion experience either have no religious or Christian background, or negative attitudes to religion have been more effectively communicated to them than positive ones. Statistics indicate that this group forms the majority of the population and in certain countries, Britain for example, many people in the group never become religiously involved with any Church or denomination. A large number of non-religious individuals have probably had no religious upbringing or significant contact with religious people. There may be, however, a number of apostates who have lost their faith as a consequence of the failure of religious education, or the success of anti-religious teaching. Attitudes can be changed in either direction by intent or mistake.

The remainder of the group become committed to the religious life through a sudden or gradual conversion experience. The background of such people may be religious or non-religious. Those individuals with a religious background may be influenced in a negative way and then, at a later date, positive influences produce either a sudden or gradual conversion. There may be several approaches and withdrawals from religious commitment before the final decision is made. This is equally true of those without a religious background, but in general their development may be characterised by less significant negative influences. It is probably the sudden convert with a non-religious background who is least influenced by the religious teacher, although even here unconscious processes may be affected by the teacher's example or arguments and may play an important part either during or after the sudden conversion experience. The gradual convert can be greatly influenced by the attitudes and arguments of the religious educator. He is the person looking for answers and he will examine any solution offered to him. But even in this case the educator can have a positive or negative influence.

The part the religious teacher can play in the development of religious commitment is different for each conversion type. In the case of the unconscious conversion type, positive solutions or attitudes are offered to the individual as problems arise. In this way religious participation and involvement are developed almost as a natural process and negative influences, if they occur, may be counteracted. The gradual convert needs more help to overcome the negative influences to religious commitment and here the teacher can play a very important part. The teacher's role is probably least significant for the sudden convert, the possible influence on the unconscious processes remains in the realms of conjecture. Once some sort of religious commitment is achieved, the teacher trying to encourage religious faith has additional responsibilities to all three conversion types. It involves providing the opportunities and the material so that religious and spiritual growth can parallel mental development. This avoids possible loss of faith by reducing areas of conflict or offering suggested solutions where the need arises. In a sense the initial teaching provided for the unconscious conversion group is now applied to all three groups. The non-religious or anti-religious teacher can have a similar affect in each of the conversion types but, of course, in a negative direction.

The religious teacher, then, has a dual role, to provide religious information and to influence religious commitment. Both must be exercised, information without commitment reduces religious education to historical or literary studies. When this is stressed it may be unwise and undesirable to expect the state to provide religious education of this nature, especially when a large section of the population does not appear to want a religious faith.

The Preacher

An examination of the role of the preacher reveals a greater concentration on commitment, not only on the initial decision to become religious but also on the continuous development of the individual in the religious life. The principal tool of the preacher is the sermon, and while the sermon occasionally may only provide information, in general its main purpose is to produce action. The maxim given to many prospective ministers during their training as preachers 'so to teach . . . that my hearers may be moved to do . . .' indicates the motivational emphasis of the sermon. The preacher is, therefore, trying to change attitudes when he draws attention to a particular area of a religious activity, points out the Christian ideal and how far short most of the congregation fall from that ideal. He will probably use all three classes of incentive discussed by Hovland et al. (1953) in order to get his point across. He will use arguments and justifications in order to try and persuade the congregation that his conclusions are correct, he will stress the advantages of acting on the advice he offers, and will emphasise the dire consequences of ignoring the conclusions he has drawn. The preacher, unlike the teacher, is not so completely committed to imparting religious information and can therefore concentrate more on trying to increase the level of participation and involvement in religious activity. In general the emotional level in preaching is much higher than one would expect to be used by the teacher. This is partly the result of the different aims of the methods of communication and partly due to the fact that whereas teaching tends to be spread over a fairly long period of time, preaching is normally restricted to two or three short periods on a Sunday. It is also worth bearing in mind the general character of the congregation. Most sermons are directed to congregations who are already, in some sense, committed to Christian belief or they would not be attending church. This means that the sermon usually attempts to increase the personal devotion of the more conventionally religious and to deepen the spiritual awareness of the genuinely devout. In terms of religious origins, the preacher plays a significant and important part in the religious development of those individuals who fall in the unconscious conversion group. The techniques employed produce an atmosphere in which the person is regularly encouraged to participate in religious activity and is given suggested solutions to problems he may have to face in the future. Such information is also invaluable to the gradual convert : here is a preacher who can be relied on to provide a positive counter-action to the negative influences that he may be experiencing in his religious life. We would not expect preaching, in normal circumstances, to result in sudden conversion, for two main reasons : first, the sermon is not exclusively designed for the purpose; and second, the congregation in general may not need this type of initial commitment.

The sermon also has great value after the religious life has begun. It provides opportunities for considering the implications of the new found faith, suggested solutions to problems the individual may expect to meet, and regular exhortation to become more deeply involved in religious activity, to change his attitudes until they conform to the Christian ideal. In this way the preacher helps to maintain the religious commitment of his congregation.

The Evangelist

The evangelist is a specialist preacher, his main aim is conversion –initial commitment to religious belief. His attention to religious information is minimal and almost all of his addresses will use the three classes of incentive which seem to be important in bringing about attitude changes. The emotional level of his speech will be very much higher than the sermon of the preacher; indeed, it may reach levels of high emotional excitement. The evangelistic technique produces the sudden convert and on occasions the culminating experience of the gradual conversion process. The evangelist needs to bear in mind that only a few individuals are susceptible to this approach while others are totally alienated from Christianity by his efforts. He also has to face the problem that about 50 per cent of the sudden converts he is instrumental in producing lose their faith. It seems desirable for evangelistic teams to use some form of selection so that the loss rate is reduced and the number of people repelled from Christianity is kept to a minimum.

At this point it is worth considering a finding of Janis and Feshbach (1953) arising from their study of fear appeals. They used three different levels of fear appeal intensity, produced by lectures pointing out the dangers of neglecting dental hygiene. The fear appeal of greatest intensity produced the largest amount of emotional tension but it did not effect any significant change in hygiene practised by the group exposed to the lecture. The greatest change in practice and the strongest resistance to counter-propaganda was produced by the fear appeal of lowest intensity.

The effects of the highly emotional preaching of evangelists like

Wesley would seem to contradict this finding. But their result may not have universal applicability since all generations do not seem to emphasise the importance of rational argument to the same extent. If their experiments had been conducted during Wesley's era, or even today, a quite different result might have been produced. The findings of Janis and Feshbach then, may have limited application, not only for different generations but for different groups within each generation (their original work was based on High School students). They have, however, drawn attention to the fact that there may not be a simple linear relationship between the intensity of fear appeals and change in attitude. ' The higher the emotion the better the results ', is a slogan that needs very careful consideration.

It has been pointed out that there is a variation in the use of fear appeals, that is stressing the dangers of ignoring the warnings of the communicator. The emotional level also varies; the evangelist uses the greatest intensity and the teacher the least. Janis and Feshbach's finding would argue for a reduction in the emotional intensity, especially at evangelistic meetings. One has to remember, however, that there are individual differences in responsiveness to fear appeals of varying intensity. It is possible that the evangelist is attracting only a small number of people because the emotional intensity level is too high for the rest of the audience. If such responsiveness is normally distributed, like most psychological characteristics, then one would expect there to be an optimum intensity level, where the majority of the population would show attitude change. This is the level that the evangelist and the preacher should use in their respective roles.

In chapter 6 it was suggested that Sargant's theory may be appropriate for explaining some of the more extreme forms of sudden conversion. His theory falls into the category described as physiological persuasion. It would seem that in most instances an evangelist is unable to produce this effect alone. His address needs to be accompanied by snake handling or formalised drug taking before states of exhaustion and increased suggestibility occur. It is possible that education has reduced the significance of fear as a tool in the hands of the evangelist. Certainly Wesley's audience and perhaps more modern, but ill-educated groups seem more susceptible to the effects of fear oratory.

SUMMARY

The main concern of the chapter has been attitude change in

religious behaviour. The effects of education and training on the development of belief were examined. Three methods of attitude change, rational, emotional and physiological were proposed and how the techniques may be applied within the area of religion was considered. Religion is propagated by teacher, preacher, and evangelist. The last part of the chapter examined their methods and suggested ways of improving their effectiveness in the light of the three types of religious conversion. It must be pointed out that these same techniques can be used to try and produce anti-religious attitudes.

Many different concepts and ideas about religion have been considered in the previous chapters, and now one task remains : an attempted evaluation and conclusion of them. This is not an easy task when there are so many conflicting research findings, and also conspicuous gaps in the available information, but despite the problems there are a number of important points that have been uncovered which offer hopes of a better understanding of religious behaviour and belief.

Religious people appear to be a distinctive group, identified by certain common beliefs and behaviour. It is this similarity between them which appears to be revealed by the finding that religious belief is uni-dimensional. The very use of the term ' religious people ' is of course assuming that this group has certain common characteristics. But with the ever-increasing amount of information becoming available it is a fact which needs to be regularly re-iterated. In contrast to this finding there is an equally basic one, that the religious population is heterogeneous. In other words, although religious people as a group have certain characteristics in common, there are many areas of belief, practice and personality where they are very different. Such differences are responsible for the existence of numerous sub-groups within the religious system. The variety of religious experience is confirmed by the finding that religious belief is multi-dimensional.

It is apparent from the discussion in previous chapters that there is no single personality or environmental factor which alone can account for all aspects of religious belief and behaviour. This conclusion seems equally applicable to the religion of the individual and of the group. The research work in the area indicates a complex situation with a multitude of causal and developmental factors associated with the phenomenon of religion. Some attempt has been made to separate out of this complexity the principal factors from those which appear to play a less significant role. This has proved no easy task. Not only is the subject matter complex but the investigator's tools seem to show a variety equalled only by religious activity itself! Conclusions must be tentative, even in areas where results have been repeatedly confirmed, since errors of sampling and the dubious validity of the questionnaires used may lead to false conclusions. The problem is highlighted by the finding of Kilpatrick et al. (1970) which indicates that the comparative dogmatism of Catholic and major Protestant Churches is dependent on the area in which the survey is carried out and the denominational composition of the Protestant group. Despite these basic limitations, and the tenuous nature of the evidence, the major conclusions that have been suggested in the previous chapters will be reiterated and discussed.

CAUSAL FACTORS OF RELIGIOUS BELIEF

Attention has already been drawn to the difficulty of determining the direction of causality. Does a given personality factor cause an individual either directly or indirectly to become religious, or are such personality factors a result of religious behaviour modifying beliefs and changing personality. Many personality traits are open to a considerably degree of change either by simple everyday environmental circumstances or by traumatic events, such as the death of a loved one or a serious accident. In some cases, a sudden conversion might be described as a traumatic event, especially if it is accompanied by some of the hysterical manifestations recorded by Davenport (1905). After such experiences some fundamental change in personality may occur. The dramatic accounts recorded about certain individuals rescued from the 'dregs of society' by Christian conversion add weight to the argument.

Obviously this makes the task of the investigator even more difficult, especially if he is trying to discover the mechanisms which produce and maintain religion by studying religious people. There appears to be two possible solutions to the problem. The first is a longitudinal study, where a large sample of the population is given an extensive battery of personality tests while they are children and later re-examined as adults in order to determine and investigate those who have subsequently become religious. One would then be able to deduce personality factors leading to the development of religious behaviour. There are obvious practical difficulties involved in this method especially retaining contact with the subjects. In addition the investigators interest in the topic has to be maintained over a number of years and in certain circumstances this might prove impossible.

There are very few longitudinal studies of religious behaviour reported in the literature, so some alternative method has to be applied in order to decide whether a variable is a cause or a consequence of religious behaviour and belief. In many cases this is an impossible task. A variable may be causal in one context but consequential in another or it may be merely associated with the causal variables. The only way round the problem seems to be to examine variables which are not significantly modified by environmental influences but are predominantly causal in their affect. The second possible solution to the problem of causality entails a closer examination of what is involved in personality. There are two factors which contribute to personality, inherited characteristics and learning and experience. The genetic variables are referred to as constitutional factors and include all our physical characteristics. These factors are not modified by learning or by changes in environmental circumstances. Therefore, if it is possible to find some common constitutional factors in a religious population, it can be concluded with far greater confidence that these are in some way responsible for the development of religious belief.

CONSTITUTIONAL FACTORS

Sex is a constitutional factor which seems to be very important in religious belief and behaviour. Women consistently show greater activity on all the various religious scales that have been used. But sex is a very complex variable, as not only are there physical and hormonal differences between male and female but each sex is expected to fulfil a quite different role in the home and in society. A number of possible explanations for the greater religious activity of women were discussed but the one which seemed most appropriate emphasised the different role each sex has in society. The female role stresses many of the virtues which form part of the Christian ethic and thus the similarity of emphasis may be primarily responsible for sex differences in levels of religious activity. The sex role is learned; it is part of our cultural heritage. In other societies the roles may be quite different; even in our own culture there is evidence that the role expected of women is changing. The female role is only partially determined by genetical inheritance and so the value of sex as a causal variable is reduced. It is possible that when an individual becomes religious there is a role modification, but it may not be the role which predisposes the person to choose religious faith. The male/female classification system is based an anatomical structure, but other measures indicate that this may be an oversimplification. There is some evidence for treating sex as a continuum with extreme masculinity and extreme femininity forming the two poles. If this is accepted and a measure of masculinity/femininity can be found which is genetically determined and independent of role play, then a significant correlation between such a measure and religious activity would indicate that sex was a vital factor in religious belief. There is, however, no evidence at the moment of any research along these lines, but perhaps the relative proportion of male and female hormones in the blood stream could form a useful area of enquiry.

Intelligence is another variable which appears to be genetically determined. Research studies, especially those comparing the intelligence of fraternal and identical twins, indicate that heredity plays a major part in intelligence. However, the same experiments also reveal that environmental factors play some part in the phenomenon although these seem to be less important than the inherited characteristics. This does mean that any conclusions derived from established correlations with intelligence will be far less clear cut than if intelligence was totally genetically determined.

Despite some conflicting results and the possibility that social factors have been inadequately controlled, general research evidence seems to indicate that religious people in general are less intelligent and that religious conservatives seem to be less intelligent than religious liberals. It might be concluded from this information that intelligence is a factor which prevents people becoming religious. Such an inference is going beyond the available evidence. There are two main points to bear in mind. The I.T.A. survey (1970) indicates that people make a clear distinction between personal and institutional religions and 29 per cent of the people who did not belong to any Church claimed they were either very or fairly religious. If the suggested negative correlation between religion and intelligence is accepted then this group of non-affiliated religious people should also be less intelligent. Further evidence is necessary to test this prediction. The survey indicates that religious belief and membership of a religious institution are not coincident. Perhaps the variable of conventionalism is important in this context : the more conventionally religious are less intelligent than the genuinely devout. Alternatively the institutionally religious could be less intelligent than those non-affiliated religious people. Both of these suggestions could mean that religious belief and intelligence are not related and conflicting results could have occurred as a result of contamination from other variables. The other main point has already been mentioned in the previous chapter, that a lower average intelligence score can occur in a number of ways. An over-representation of the middle and lower intelligence individuals could produce the same effect as an under-representation of very intelligent people. Some further research work is necessary in this area. If there is the same proportion of highly intelligent individuals in both the religious group and the general population, then factors apart from intelligence could be responsible for the research findings. The explanation that the more intelligent person is less likely to conform to traditional beliefs seems adequate justification for the finding that religious conservatives are less intelligent than religious liberals.

At this point it becomes apparent that there are relatively few clear-cut constitutional factors. Most variables, naturally enough, are a combination of inherited and acquired characteristics and often it is impossible to separate the two. In addition there are relatively few variables having significant affects on behaviour which have a large genetic component. In terms of behaviour early upbringing seems to have a far greater influence than genetics. There are, however, a few other constitutional factors that should be considered.

Eysenck (1947) offers two variables which he insists are, to a considerable degree, determined by hereditary factors. These are his two dimensions of Neuroticism and Extraversion/Introversion, both of which, he claims, are independent of intelligence. If these variables are principally constitutional factors some significant conclusions should be forthcoming.

Neuroticism scales have usually indicated that religious people gain slightly higher scores than the general population, but there are also intra-group differences in neuroticism. This would seem to indicate that neuroticism may be an important variable for parts of the religious population but not necessarily for every religious person. If neuroticism is a measure of emotionality (the general level of emotional response to a given stimulus), then one might expect those individuals who normally respond at a high emotional level to be members of churches where there is a high level of emotional release in their services. Such churches tend to be fundamentalist in character and therefore the members would be predominantly religious conservatives. Using this argument one can predict that religious conservatives will have higher neuroticism scores. There is some evidence that this is true but considerably more research is required. The possible importance of neuroticism in sudden conversion and the fact that sudden converts are predominantly religious conservatives would lead to the same conclusion but there is little evidence as yet available to indicate significant differences in neuroticism for the types of conversion experience.

Turning to the extraversion/introversion dimension there is a similar pattern, religious people seeming to be more introverted but there are again intra-group differences. Introversion may be an important variable in all three types of conversion experience and thus one would expect higher introversion scores in the religious group as a whole. It is also possible that intra-group differences are the result of variation along the religious conventionalism continuum, the more conventional being less introverted. These suggestions are very tentative especially when Brown's (1962) finding that the personality variable factor (including neuroticism and extraversion/introversion is independent of the religious belief factor, is borne in mind. Brown's result is indeed important, for up to this point significant correlations had been reported between religious belief and certain personality variables. One reason for these conflicting results may be the differences between the samples of religious people studied. Brown used psychology students at Adelaide University, whereas other investigators have examined specific religious groups, for example Gilmore (1969) on Pentecostalists, McCarthy (1942) on Roman Catholics. The basic problem is to find out the reason for the different results; the most likely cause seems to lie in the selection of the groups for study.

One constitutional factor of a somewhat different nature is age. Instead of exerting a constant influence on behaviour like most constitutional factors, it exerts a variable but systematic influence on the individual. A considerable amount of evidence has accumulated indicating that older people are more religious. Again a number of reasons for the finding were discussed but the most likely explanation for the increase in religious activity with age had two important aspects. The first point is a purely practical one : older people, especially when their families have grown up and left home, have more time to follow their religious interests. This, however, does not explain the increase in religious belief with age, in particular an increasing belief in immortality. The problem of religious belief leads to the second aspect, the application of the frustration theory to the fear of death. Individuals seem to anticipate frustration when they contemplate death, for death implies a cessation of all the satisfaction of life with no guarantee of anything to follow in compensation for the loss. Equally frustrating is the expected decline in ability with advancing age. As people get older the problem of death and senility become a more significant threat and many individuals find solace in the religious concepts of immorality, heavenly bliss, and a new spiritual body. The increase of religious interest stimulated by fear and facilitated by the greater availability of free time seems to result in increased religious activity.

There may be an increase in personal belief without any apparent increase in religious activity like church attendance. Cavan (1949) found that while 100 per cent of men between 90–94 years believed in an after-life only 50 per cent had favourable attitudes towards religion. This finding seems to emphasis the distinction between personal and institutional religion, where an increase in religious beliefs may not necessarily lead to greater support for organised religion.

The conclusions arising from the five constitutional variables that have been considered need to be seen in the framework of the multi-dimensional character of religious belief. In other words some of the factors may be important in causing the development of religious beliefs of one kind but not of another. So we can broadly conclude that women, especially those who readily accept the traditional female role seem to be generally more religious. Age may have a more profound affect on personal rather than institutional religion, especially in men. Lower intelligence and higher neuroticism may facilitate the development of religious conservatism or predispose the individual to experience sudden conversion, while higher intelligence seems to bring about the growth of radical and unorthodox religious beliefs. Finally the extraversion/introversion dimension may be related to religious conventionalism, extraverts being more conventional in their religious beliefs and allegiances. Most of these general conclusions need further verification; they indicate areas in which additional research is necessary and where fruitful results may be attained.

NON-CONSTITUTIONAL FACTORS

The variables considered so far seem to have a causal influence on religion because they are genetically determined and thus formed prior to the development of religious belief. The direction of causality of the variables considered in this next section cannot be so easily established. It is difficult to determine whether they influence religious beliefs or religious beliefs influence them.

It has been suggested that the attitude to authority is an important aspect of authoritarianism and dogmatism. Religious people are asked to submit to divine authority and sometimes clerical authority. This could be the main reason why their scores on the two variables are higher than those of the general population. But many of the questions in the scales do not have a particularly religious quality. Why should religious people be authoritarian or dogmatic on issues outside of religion and ethics? One could argue that no issue is outside the scope of religion, for religion embraces the whole of life. Therefore these tests require separate norms for religious people, and comparisons with non-religious groups are undesirable. This seems a very extreme attitude, for while religion affects the whole of life there are issues which are left to the individual's discretion without any directives from religious institutions. In these areas one might anticipate that religious people would be no more authoritarian or dogmatic than the general population. A detailed analysis of the items in each scale is necessary in order to determine the questions which contribute most to their high scoring. If such items have a religious significance and their score on other items is within the normal range then the hypothesis would be verified. Despite the plausibility of this explanation there are certain indications that this is not the case. For example ethnocentrism is highly correlated with authoritarianism but only asks questions to do with racial prejudice. Why should religious people score higher on scales of racial prejudice? The finding that this applies particularly to the conventionally religious is only partially satisfactory. Aggression directed at the out-groups in order to defend the in-group, in this case the religious institution, seems applicable only when the out-group poses a threat. But some racial groups pose no such threat and indeed a large percentage of the group may be part of the in-group, that is they belong to the same denomination. At this point we may begin to favour the alternative direction of influence, a personality factor which influences religious activity, as well as other important areas on behaviour, producing authoritarian attitudes in religion, politics and other social relationships. The high correlation between religions and political conservatism tends to substantiate this suggestion but the importance of social class in this particular relationship should not be overlooked. There is no need to select one direction of influence in preference to another, since both may be operating, one substantiating and reinforcing the other. Indeed it is still possible to maintain that the development of what may be called religious authoritarianism may modify the personality to produce authoritarianism in other attitude areas.

The significant affect that social class has on a number of vari-

F

ables emphasises the importance of early environment and training for the individual. Social class affects political attitudes and more profoundly voting behaviour, but its influence on religious conservatism is less clear. It woud appear that upper class people support conservative political parties but may be more radical in their religious beliefs. The suggestion has been made that there is an underlying personality trait of conservatism and this normally determines the political and religious attitudes of the individual, except that the type of conversion experience can overrule the ideology : sudden converts tend to become religious conservatives while the gradual or unconscious conversion experience, more often results in religious liberalism.

One remaining factor needs comment, namely suggestibility. Religious conservatives seem to score high on tests of prestige suggestibility. This fact may again be related to group cohesive forces. The group affords support for beliefs, so to conform to the group provides additional social support. Beliefs outside the realm of empirical verification seem to need greater social support for their maintenance. Religious conservatives who may be less intelligent may in consequence need greater social support than the more intelligent religious liberals. The imponderable problem remains : do the religious conservatives who learn to accept social support for their religious beliefs, in consequence, also seek social support in other attitudinal areas, or does suggestibility influence the development of both religious and non-religious attitudes? The finding that extreme Protestant groups are susceptible to primary suggestion may indicate another necessary mechanism in suddden conversion, especially in the extremely emotional type.

THE ORIGIN OF RELIGION

The origin of religion is an important area, although its consideration is outside the realm of psychology. It is to sociology that we look to suggest the significance and purpose that religion may have in maintaining the societies and institutions of our own age. In other words, religious institutions contribute in some way to the necessary equilibrium of society, or they promise spiritual rewards as a substitute for material prosperity to the more deprived sectors of society. It is left to anthropology to discuss the origins of early religion and here two explanations seem plausible : the first concerns man's attempt to understand the world in which he lived; and the second the way he tried to allay the fear of objects outside of his control in what for him was a threatening environment. It is obvious that most theologians would accept this only as an explanation of early religions, when man was seeking God. They would make a distinction between primitive religion and Christianity which in essence is God revealing Himself to man.

CONVERSION

More closely related to psychology is the origin of religious belief within the individual. The three conversion types described in chapter 4, while not covering all aspects provide an interesting way of identifying the main routes to religious belief, especially for Christians. In chapter 6 it was suggested that (1) unconscious conversion subjects were a product of social learning; (2) various conflicts or frustrations in the environment contribute to the gradual converts experience, while (3) those who are more suggestible or subjected to physiological persuasion may experience a sudden conversion. In many of the preceeding chapters the importance of religious experience, especially conversion, has been emphasised. It has been suggested that the type of conversion experience is significantly related to most other areas of religious belief and behaviour. The direction of causation however is not easily determined although it can be assumed that as in many cases it represents the beginning of religious development, then it will influence religious belief. But we have seen that in certain circumstances religious belief can predispose an individual to experience a sudden conversion. Despite this fact there seems little doubt that an individual's conversion experience is of great significance for his subsequent religious activity. The three basic conversion types studied by Scobie (1967) are a little more tentative. Although he claims that all subjects chose one of the three types in order to describe their personal experience, he does draw attention to different basic attitudes to conversion which might result in five categories rather than three. There is also the possibility that only two categories are significant, namely those who regard conversion as a once-for-all experience and those who consider it a continuous process (although he found that this was a less significant division than that for conversion experience). Another possibility is that the use of the term conversion is obscuring some of the similarities of the religious experience. If a term equally acceptable to all religious people could be found the results might be more illuminating. This area obviously needs further research but the investigation of Scobie does indicate the vital importance of the conversion experience and its significance in the religious life of the individual.

There are certain significant characteristics associated with the three conversion types, but perhaps the clearest picture that emerges concerns the sudden convert. Certain personality factors such as neuroticism, introversion and suggestibility seems to facilitate the occurrence of the experience. Parental commitment to the need for sudden conversion and attendance at evangelistic meetings must also be seen as important factors determining a sudden conversion experience. The experience appears to be associated with a number of variables. Sudden converts are usually personally involved in their religion and thus will have low scores on measures of conventionalism. Usually their scores on religious conservatism will be high because of the character of evangelical teaching which encourages sudden conversion. Scores on authoritarianism and dogmatism will be high also, especially if such scales are loaded on religious or political conservatism. The conservative beliefs of sudden converts tend to persist even when they experience training of a more liberal character.

The other two conversion types are less clearly defined. The dimension on conventionalism may be used to try and clarify the situation. Those who score high on conventionalism are probably well satisfied with the material advantage that church membership may bring. They may find a certain sense of security in supporting the establishment. Many may have acquired their attachment to conventional religious values from their parents who were either conventionally religious themselves or only succeeded in passing on the conventional habits of religion but not the personal commitment. They may not be deeply involved with church doctrine and may thus repeat without conviction traditional beliefs given to them or their lack of involvement may enable them to challenge traditional views and accept most radical ideas. In general, such people would probably claim an unconscious conversion experience although a few may have acquired their conventional values later in life and thus may talk of a gradual conversion. The development of their religious beliefs is predominantly governed by non-religious factors. It is the non-religious values which influence and modify the religious belief rather than, as in the case of the sudden and gradual convert, the religious beliefs influencing other values and attitudes.

Those individuals who are low scorers on the conventionalism dimension, that is those who are personally involved in religious belief, will resemble sudden converts. Introversion may be an important variable, but neuroticism and suggestibility may be less important. Such people will usually claim to be gradual converts although there may be some individuals who have acquired a similar personal commitment to their parents and may thus claim an unconscious conversion experience.

In general they will be less conservative in their beliefs than the sudden converts because they have not accepted a particular doctrinal position as part of their conversion, but have thought through very carefully some specific issues and perhaps achieved certain compromise positions on them. Such compromises would produce a more radical score. But because of their personal commitment to religious beliefs, they will rarely develop the same extensive radical scores as those that gain high scores in conventionalism.

As they have come to religious belief through a rational and logical evaluation of the arguments we could expect their religious beliefs, unlike the sudden convert, to be profoundly influenced by the teaching and training they receive.

It would seem that the religious population can be divided into the conventionally religious (predominantly unconscious conversion subjects) and the genuinely devout. The genuinely devout in the main are either sudden or gradual converts. This broad typology is probably only a rough approximation, but given some interval measure of conversion experience, there would probably be a high correlation between it and the measures of conventionalism.

THE DECLINE OF CHRISTIANITY IN WESTERN SOCIETY

The comments on conventionalism leads us to a consideration of the intrinsic/extrinsic dimension which purports to distinguish between the genuinely devout and the conventionally religious. This topic needs to be considered in detail because it may help in understanding the decreasing support that many Christian denominations are experiencing at the moment. The membership statistics (see Table 7) for the major denominations in Britain, indicate a slight decline in support, with the exception of the Roman Catholic Church. The population of Britain has increased by about 2 per cent over the period 1961-71 and this increase is reflected to some extent by the slight increase in baptised members of the Church of England. Confirmation may be a more accurate indicator of membership in the Anglican Church, and this does follow the downward trend experienced by most other denominations. These figures contrast with those for the U.S.A. where all the denominations have increased in size over the same period. However, the population of the nation has increased by 13.3 per cent during the ten-year period, whereas the religious proportion only increased 12.9 per cent, showing therefore a slight decline in the proportion of the population who have some form of religious commitment. The overall picture, then, is a significant decline in church membership in Britain, despite an increase in population; whereas in the U.S.A. there is a very slight relative decline for the population as a whole. Church attendance figures present a similar picture. One possible explanation for the difference between the nations could be the nature of the churches themselves. American churches seem to be more socially orientated, providing many social activities for their members. This is much less true of their British counterparts who concentrate more on worship. It is possible that a decrease in religious belief has been successfully concealed in American churches by their concentrating on social activities.

TABLE 7: MEMBERSHIP OF DENOMINATIONS IN BRITAIN AND U.S.A.
IN THOUSANDS

	1970*	1966*	1960*
BRITAIN			
Church of England			
Baptised	27,736	27,658	27,323
Confirmation	9,510	9,960	9,792
Episcopal Church of Scotland	84	93	97
Roman Catholic			
England		4,000	3,660
Scotland		810	793
Methodist	759	773	1,105
Presbyterian			
Church of Scotland	1,110	1,220	1,292
England		65	71
U.S.A.			
Roman Catholic	48,215	47,468	42,876
Episcopal		3,420	3,269
Methodist		13,693	12,632
Presbyterian		4,406	4,327
Lutheran		8,999	8,304
Baptist		25,899	21,396
Church of Christ		4,143	4,000
Protestant	71,715	69,268	64,474
TOTAL	131,046	126,444	116,109

* These years are only approximate as denominations collect their statistics at different times.
(abstracted from *The Statesman's Year Book*).

There are other indications that established religious institutions are proving less attractive to the population, especially the younger generation. In American and Britain there is an increasing interest in the mystical and Eastern religions, magic and hallucinagenic drugs. It would appear that these are people searching for satisfaction outside of the established religious denominations. These activities seem to represent a search for new experiences, or even perhaps a search for meaning and purpose. In times past the denominations seem to have been able to give meaning and purpose to most of the population, but perhaps this is not the case at the present time. It seems that religious or spiritual needs still exist for a large proportion of the population, but organised religion seems unable to meet their needs. The I.T.A. Survey (1970) indicated that among those who claimed to belong to no religious group, 29 per cent described themselves as fairly or very religious. An indication that at least for this group the denominations fail to meet their spiritual requirements or, alternatively are not seen as relevant.

Another possible explanation relates to the distinction between the genuinely devout and the conventionally religious. It is possible that the attractiveness of church membership and attendance as a conventional activity has decreased more in Britain than America, and therefore the proportion of conventionally religious may be less in the British population. The decline in church membership might be a consequence of a fall in conventional religion, rather than a reduction in the number of genuinely devout. A comparison in conventionality between random samples of American and British religious people might indicate the validity or otherwise of the assertion.

The relationship between personality and religious belief must remain an open question. Early studies seem to indicate a number of correlates, but more recent factor analytic work suggests that religious belief is independent of personality. Such findings may again be due to differences in sample. Large heterogeneous groups may give an independence between personality and the uni-dimensional factor of religion. In homogeneous groups where the multi-dimensional nature of religion is indicated, then personality might be an important aspect of belief. It is also possible that personality may be more important in determining the type of conversion experience. These suggestions however, need to be experimentally verified but they could help to resolve some of the conflicting evidence that exists at the moment.

The final conclusion must be that although there seems to be a considerable amount of experimental data, there is a marked absence of an overall theoretical framework. If any significant advance is to be made in our understanding of religion then an adequate theory of religion must be constructed. As yet such a theory does not exist.

FUTURE DEVELOPMENTS

It is impossible to make accurate predictions about the future development of a subject but the area in which progress is antici- pated can be indicated. There are at least three topics where some development can be expected.

A reference was made in chapter 3 to the 'third force' in psychology. One would hope that a scientific examination in this area of such topics as freedom, responsibility, suffering, death, and the meaning of life, would prove fruitful especially as they are vital questions to most religious organisations. Such studies should produce a clearer understanding of religious belief and behaviour and demonstrate the value of the approach of existential psychology.

It would be unwise to ignore the considerable research work that has been carried out within the domain of our second topic, namely social psychology and sociology. One must anticipate a continuation of these valuable investigations and therefore the development of ideas about the value and significance of 'group' religion – especially with reference to its interaction with society and its influence on the individual.

The final topic which seems to be of considerable importance concerns the interaction and structure of attitudes. It has long been known that there are correlations between certain sets of attitudes, for instance people who are conservative in their religious attitudes usually hold conservative political attitudes. Two recent books, *Beliefs, Attitudes and Values* by Rokeach (1968) and *The Psycho- logy of Conservatism* by Wilson (1973), indicate that this topic is now receiving extensive examination. Available information to date would suggest that each individual has a prevailing ideology, either conservative or radical, which influences attitudes held in many areas. It does seem possible however that in certain cases a specific set of attitudes may be independent of the prevailing ideology. Such independence may be mediated by a dramatic conversion experi- ence. For example individuals with a prevailing radical ideology may be conservative in their religious beliefs as a consequence of their sudden conversion.

In conclusion it must be pointed out that a fuller understanding of the problems of the psychology of religion can only be made if both its similarities to other attitudes structures and its distinctive qualities are investigated. The development suggested above augers well for the future of this vital and interesting subject.

Bibliography

ADORNO, T. W., FRENKEL-BRUNSWIK, E., LEVINSON, D. J. and SANDFORD, R. N. (1950), *The Authoritarian Personality*, Harper.

ALLEN, E. H., and HITES, R. W. (1961), 'Factors in religious attitudes in older adolescents', *Journal of Social Psychology*, vol. 55, pp. 265-73.

ALLISON, J. (1967), 'Adaptive regression and intense religious experiences', *Journal of Nervous and Mental Disease*, vol. 145 (6), pp. 452-63.

ALLPORT, G. W. (1954), *The Nature of Prejudice*, Addison-Wesley.

ALLPORT, G. W. (1955), *Becoming*, Yale University Press.

ALLPORT, G. W., GILLESPIE, J. M., and YOUNG, J. (1948), 'The religion of the post-war college student', *Journal of Psychology*, vol. 25, pp. 3-33.

ALLPORT, G. W., and KRAMER, B. M. (1946), 'Some roots of prejudice', *Journal of Psychology*, vol. 22, pp. 9-39.

ALLPORT, G. W., and ROSS, J. M. (1967), 'Personal religious orientation and prejudice', *Journal of Personality and Social Psychology*, vol. 5 (4), pp. 432-43.

ALLPORT, G. W., VERNON, P. E., and LINDZEY, G. (1960), *Study of Values: Manual*, Houghton Mifflin.

AMON, J., and YELA, M. (1968), 'Dimensions de la religiosidad', *Revista de Psicologia General y Aplicada*, vol. 23 (95), pp. 989-93.

ARGYLE, M. A. (1958), *Religious Behaviour*, Routledge and Kegan Paul.

ARSENIAN, S. (1943), 'Change in evaluative attitudes during four years of college', *Journal of Applied Psychology*, vol. 27, pp. 338-49.

BENDER, I. I. (1958), 'Changes in religious interest', *Journal of Abnormal and Social Psychology*, vol. 57, pp. 41-6.

BERKOWITZ, W. R. (1967), 'Use of the Sensation-seeking Scale with Thai subjects', *Psychological Reports*, vol. 20, pp. 635-41.

BETTS, G. (1929), *The Beliefs of 700 Ministers*, Abingdon.

BOCOCK, R. J. (1970), 'The Role of the Anglican Clergyman', *Social Compass*, vol. 17 (4), pp. 533-44.

BOISEN, A. T. (1955), *Religion in Crisis and Custom*, Harper.

BRANDON, O. (1960), *Battle for the Soul: Aspects of Religious Conversion*, Hodder and Stoughton.

BROEN, W. E. (1957), 'A factor-analytic study of religious attitudes', *Journal of Abnormal and Social Psychology*, vol. 54, pp. 176-9.

BROWN, D. G., and LOWE, W. L. (1951), 'Religious beliefs and personality characteristics of college students', *Journal of Social Psychology*, vol. 33, pp. 103-29.

BROWN, L. B. (1962), 'A study of religious belief', *British Journal of Psychology*, vol. 53, pp. 259-72.

BROWN, L. B. (1964). 'Towards a classification of religious orientation', *Journal for the Scientific Study of Religion*, vol. 4, pp. 91-9.

BROWN, L. B. (1965), 'Aggression and denominational membership', *British Journal of Social and Clinical Psychology*, vol. 4, pp. 175-8.

BROWN, I. B. (1966), 'The structure of religious belief', *Journal for the Scientific Study of Religion*, vol. 5, pp. 259-72.

BROWN, L. B., and PALLANT, D. J. (1962), 'Religious belief and social pressure', *Psychological Reports*, vol. 10, pp. 813-14.

BULTMAN, R., (1963), *The History of the Synoptic Tradition*, Oxford, Blackwell.

BURCHINAL, L. G. (1957), 'Marital satisfaction and religious behaviour', *American Sociological Review*, vol. 22, pp. 306-10.

BURTT, H. E., and FALKENBURG, D. R. (1941), 'The influence of majority and expert opinion on religious attitudes', *Journal of Social Psychology*, vol. 14, pp. 269-78.

BUTLER, D., and STOKES, D. (1969), *Political Change in Britain*, Macmillan.

CARLOS, S. (1970), 'Religious participation and the urban-suburban continuum', *American Journal of Sociology*, vol. 75 (5), pp. 742-59.

CARLSON, H. B. (1934), 'Attitudes of undergraduate students', *Journal of Social Psychology*, vol. 5, pp. 202-12.

CARLSON, H. B. (1961), 'The relationship of the acute confusional state to ego development', *International Journal of Psychoanalysis*, vol. 42, pp. 517-36.

CAVAN, R. S. (1971), 'Attitude of Jewish college students in the U.S. towards inter-religious marriage', *International Journal of the Sociology of the Family*, vol. 1, Special Issue, pp. 84-98.

CEASARMAN, F. C. (1957), 'Religious conversion of sex offenders during psychotherapy', *Journal of Pastoral Care*, vol. 11, pp. 25-35.

CHRISTENSEN, C. W. (1963), 'Religious conversion', *Archives of General Psychiatry*, vol. 9 (3), pp. 207-16.

CLARK, E. T. (1928), *The Psychology of Religious Awakening*, Macmillian.

CLARK, E. T. (1949), *The Small Sects in America*, Abingdon-Cokesbury.

CLARK, W. H. (1958), *The Psychology of Religion: An Introduction to Religious Experience and Behaviour*, Macmillan.

CLAYTON, R. A. (1971), '5-D or I?', *Journal for the Scientific Study of Religion*, vol. 10 (1), pp. 37-40.

CLINE, V. B., and RICHARDS, J. M. (1965), 'A factor-analytic study of religious belief and behaviour', *Journal of Personality and Social Psychology*, vol. 1 (6), pp. 569-78.

COATES, T. J. (1973), 'Personality correlates of religious commitment: a further verification', *Journal of Social Psychology*, vol. 89 (1), pp. 159-60.

COE, G. A. (1916), *The Psychology of Religion*, University of Chicago Press.

COHN, W. (1967), 'A movie of experimentally-produced glossolalia', *Journal for the Scientific Study of Religion*, vol. 6 (2), p. 278.

COLQUHOUN, F. (1965), *Harringay Story*, Hodder and Stoughton.

CUADRA, C. A. (1953), 'A Psychometric investigation of control factors in psychological adjustment', Ph.D. dissertation, *University of California*.

DAVENPORT, F. M. (1906), *Primitive Traits in Religious Revivals*, Macmillan.

DAVIDSON, J. D. (1972), 'Patterns of Belief at the Denominational and Congregational levels', *Review of Religious Research*, vol. 13 (3), pp. 197-205.

DICE, L. R., CLARK, P. J., and GILBERT, R. I. (1965), 'Relation of fertility to religious affiliation and to church attendance in Ann Arbor, Michigan', *Eugenics Quarterly*, vol. 12 (2), pp. 102-11.

DITTES, J. E. (1969), 'Psychology of Religion', in LINDZEY G., AND ARONSON, E. (eds.), *Handbook of Social Psychology*, vol 5, Adison-Wesley.

DREGER, R. M. (1952), 'Some personality correlates of religious attitudes as determined by projective techniques', *Psychological Monographs*, vol. 66, no. 3.

DI GUISEPPE, R. A. (1971), 'Dogmatism correlation with strength of religious conviction', *Psychological Reports*, vol. 28 (1), p. 64.

DURKHEIM, E. (1897), *Suicide*, translation by SPAULDING, J. A. and SIMPSON, G., Routledge and Kegan Paul.

DURKHEIM, E. (1947), *The Elementary Forms of the Religious Life*, translation by SWAIN, J. W., The Free Press.

EDDY, J. P. (1968), 'Report of religious activities at Harvard and Radcliffe', *College Student Survey*, vol. 2 (2), pp. 31-4.

ESTUS, C. W., and OVERINGTON, M. A. (1970), 'The meaning and end of religiosity', *American Journal of Sociology*, vol. 75 (5), pp. 760-78.

EYSENCK, H. J. (1944), 'General social attitudes', *Journal of Social Psychology*, vol. 19, pp. 207-27.

EYSENCK, H. J. (1947), *Dimensions of Personality*, Routledge and Kegan Paul.

EYSENCK, H. J. (1953), *The Structure of Human Personality*, Methuen.

EYSENCK, H. J. (1954), *Psychology of Politics*, Routledge and Kegan Paul.

FAULKNER, J. E., and DEJONG, D. T. (1966), 'Religiosity in 5-D: an empirical analysis', *Social Forces*, 45, pp. 246-54.

FERGUSON, L. W. (1939), 'Primary social attitudes', *Journal of Psychology*, vol. 8, pp. 217-23.

FERGUSON, L. W. (1940), 'The measurement of primary social attitudes', *Journal of Psychology*, vol. 10, pp. 199-205.

FERGUSON, L. W. (1942), 'The isolation and measurement of nationalism', *Journal of Psychology*, vol. 16, pp. 215-28.

FERGUSON, L. W. (1944), 'Socio-psychological correlates of the primary attitude scales: I. Religionism; II. Humanitarianism', *Journal of Social Psychology*, vol. 19, pp. 81-98.

FERM, R. O. (1959), *The Psychology of Christian Conversion*, Revell.

FESTINGER, L, (1954), 'A theory of social comparison processes', *Human Relations*, vol. 7, pp. 117-40.

FESTINGER, L. (1957), *A Theory of Cognitive Dissonance*, Row, Peterson and Company.

FESTINGER, L., RIECKEN, H. W. and SCHACHTER, S. *When Prophesy Fails*, University of Minnesota Press.

FETTER, G. C. (1964), 'A comparative study of attitudes of Christian and Moslem Lebanese villagers', *Journal for the Scientific Study of Religion*, vol. 4 (1), pp. 48-59.

FISCHER, H., and HOLL, A, (1968), 'Attitude envers la religion et L'église en Autriche enquête auprès de soldats de l'armée autrichienne', *Social Compass*, vol. 15, pp. 13-35.

FISHER, S. C. (1948), 'Relationships in attitudes, opinions and values among family members', University of California Pub. Cult. Soc., vol. 2, pp. 29-100.

FLEW, A., and MACINTYRE, A. (1955), *New Essays in Philosophical Theology*, S.C.M. Press.

FLOWER, J. C. (1927), *An Approach to the Psychology of Religion*, Routledge and Kegan Paul.

FLUGEL, J. C. (1945), *Man, Morals and Society*, Duckworth.

FRAZER, J. (1929), *The Golden Bough: A Study in Magic and Religion*, London.

FREUD, S. (1907), 'Obsessive acts and religious practices', *Collected Papers*, vol. 2, pp. 25-35.

FREUD, S. (1927), *The Future of an Illusion*, Hogarth Press.

FREUD, S. (1933), *New Introductory Lectures on Psychoanalysis*. Hogarth Press.

FREUD, S. (1939), *Civilisation and its Discontents*, Hogarth Press.

FRY, C. L. (1933), 'The religious affiliations of American leaders', *Scientific Monthly*, vol. 36, pp. 241-9.

GIBBONS, D., and DE JARNETT, J. (1972), 'Hypnotic susceptibility and religious experience', *Journal for the Scientific Study of Religion*, vol. 11 (2), pp. 152-6.

GILMORE, S. K. (1969), 'Personality differences between high and low dogmatism groups of Pentecostal believers', *Journal for the Scientific Study of Religions*, vol. 8, pp. 161-6.

GLOCK, C. Y., and STARK, R. (1965), *Religion and Society in Tension*, Rand McNally.

GOLDMAN, R. (1964), *'Religious Thinking from Childhood to Adolescence'*, Routledge and Kegan Paul.

GOLDMAN, R. (1965), 'The application of Piaget's scheme of operational thinking to religious story data by means of the Guttman scalogram', *British Journal of Educational Psychology*, vol. 35 (2), pp. 158-70.

GOODE, E. (1966), 'Social class and church participation', *American Journal of Sociology*, vol. 72, pp. 102-11.

GOODE, E. (1970), 'Another look at social class and church participation: reply to Estus and Overington', *American Journal of Sociology*, vol 75 (5), pp. 779-81.

GORER, G. (1955), *Exploring English Character*, Cresset.

GREELEY, A. M. (1963), *Religion and Career*, Sheed and Ward.

GREELEY, A. M. (1965), 'The religious behaviour of graduate students', *Journal for Scientific Study of Religion*, vol. 5, pp. 34-40.

GREELEY, A. M. (1969), 'Continuities in research on the "religious factor"', *American Journal of Sociology*, vol. 75 (3), pp. 355-9.

HARLOW, H. F. (1959), 'Love in Infant Monkeys', *Scientific American*.

HARMS, E. (1944), 'The development of religious experiences in children', *American Journal of Sociology*, vol. 50, pp. 112-22.

HIGHET, J. (1957), 'The churches of Glasgow', *British Weekly*, Aug. 22nd and 29th.

HOGE, D. R. (1972), 'A validated intrinsic religious motivation scale', *Journal for Scientific Study of Religion*, vol. 11 (4), pp. 369-76.

HOGE, D. R., and CARROLL, J. W. (1973), 'Religiosity and prejudice in northern and southern churches', *Journal for the Scientific Study of Religion*, vol. 12 (2), pp. 181-97.

HOPPE, R. A. (1969), 'Religious belief and the learning of paired associates', *Journal of Social Psychology*, vol. 78 (2), pp. 275-9.

HOVLAND, C. I., JANIS, I. L., and KELLY, H. H. (1953), *Communication and Persuasion*, Yale University Press.

HOWELLS, T. H. (1928), 'A comparative study of those who accept as against those who reject religious authority'. *University of Iowa Studies: Study of Character*, vol. 2, no. 2.

HUNT, R. A., (1972), 'Mythological – symbolic religious commitment: the LAM scales, *Journal for the Scientific Study of Religion*, vol. 11 (1), pp. 42-52.

HUNT, R. A., and KING, M. B. (1971), 'The intrinsic and extrinsic concept: a review and evaluation', *Journal for the Scientific Study of Religion*, vol. 10 (4), pp. 339-56.

Independent Television Authority (1970), *Religion in Britain and Northern Ireland*.

JACKSON, E. F., FOX. W. S., and CROCKETT, H. J. (1970), 'Religious and occupational achievement', *American Sociological Review*, vol. 35 (1), pp. 48-63.

JAMES, W, (1902), *The Varieties of Religious Experience*, Longmans.

JANIS, I. L., and FESBACH, S. (1953), 'Effects of fear-arousing communications', *Journal of Abnormal and Social Psychology*, vol. 48, pp. 78-92.

JONES, W. L. (1937), *A Psychological Study of Religious Conversion*, Epworth Press.

JUNG, C. G. (1938), *Psychology and Religion*, Yale University Press.

JUNG, C. G. (1953), *Von den Wurzeln des Bewusstseins: Studien über den Archetypus*, Rascher.

JUNG, C. G. (1958), *Psychology and Religion, West and East*, Panthean Books.

KAY, W. (1968), *Moral Development*, Allen and Unwin.

KELLY, J. G., FERSON, J. E., and HOLTZMAN, W. H. (1958), 'The Measurement of attitudes towards the Negro in the South', *Journal of Social Psychology*, vol. 48. pp. 305-17.

Bibliography 175

KILDAHL, J. P. (1972), *The Psychology of Speaking in Tongues*, Harper and Row.

KILPATRICK, D. G., SUTKER, L. W., and SUTKER, P. B. (1970), 'Dogmatism, religion and religiosity, a review and re-evaluation', *Psychological Reports*, vol. 26, pp. 15-22.

KING, M. B. (1967), 'Measuring the religious variables; nine proposed dimensions', *Journal for the Scientific Study of Religion*, vol. 6, pp. 173-90.

KING, M. B., and HUNT, R. A. (1972), 'Measuring the religious variable: reflections, *Journal for Scientific Study of Religion*, vol 11 (3), pp. 240-51.

KING, S. H., and FUNKENSTEIN, D. H. (1957), 'Religious practice and cardiovascular reactions during stress', *Journal of Abnormal and Social Psychology*, vol. 55, pp. 135-7.

KIRSCHNER, R., MCGARRY, J. L., and MOORE, C. W. (1962), 'A Comparison of differences among several religious groups of children on various measures of the Rosenzweig Picture-Frustration Study', *Journal of Clinical Psychology*, vol. 18 (3), pp. 352-3.

KITAY, P. M. (1947), 'Radicalism and conservatism towards conventional religion: a psychological study based on a group of Jewish college students,' *Teachers College Contributions to Education*, no. 919.

KNAPP, R. H., and GOODRICH, H. B. (1951), 'The origins of American Scientists', *Science*, vol. 113, pp. 543-5.

LANDIS, J. T. (1949), 'Marriages of mixed and non-mixed religious faith', *American Sociological Review*, vol. 14, pp. 401-7.

LANG, A. (1898), *The Making of Religion*, London.

LAZARSFELD, P. F., BERELSON, B., and GAUDET, H. (1944), *The People's Choice*, Duell, Sloan and Pearce.

LENSKI, G. E. (1953), 'Social correlates of religious interest', *American Sociological Review*, vol. 18, pp. 533-44.

LENSKI, G. E. (1960), *The Religious Factor*, Doubleday.

LEROY, A. (1922), *The Religion of the Primitives*, New York, Macmillan.

LEUBA, J. H. (1925), *The Psychology of Religious Mysticism*, Routledge and Kegan Paul.

LEUBA, J. H. (1934), 'Religious beliefs of American scientists', *Harpers Magazine*, vol. 169, p. 297.

LIPSET, S. M., LAZARSFELD, P. F., BARTON, A. H., and LINZ, J. (1954), 'The psychology of voting: an analysis of political behaviour', in LINDZEY, G. (ed), *Handbook of Social Psychology, Vol II: Special Fields and Applications*, Addison-Wesley.

LONDON, P., SCHULIAN, R. E., and BLACK, M. S. (1964), 'Religion, guilt and ethical standards', *Journal of Social Psychology*, vol. 63, pp. 145-59.

LONG, B. H. (1965), 'Catholic-Protestant differences in acceptance of others', *Sociology and Social Research*, vol. 49, pp. 166-72.

MCCARTHY, T. J. (1942), 'Personality traits of seminarians', *Studies in Psychology and Psychiatry from the Catholic University of America*, vol. 5, no. 4, pp. 46-229.

MCCLELAND, D. C. (1961), *The Achieving Society*, Van Nostrand.

MCCONAHAY, J. B., and HOUGH, J. C. (1973), 'Love and guilt-oriented dimensions of Christian belief ', *Journal for Scientific Study of Religion*, vol. 12 (1), pp. 53-64.

MACGREGOR, G. (1960), *Introduction to Religious Philosophy*, Macmillan.

MACLEAN, A. H. (1930), 'The idea of God in Protestant religious education ', *Contributions to Education*, no. 411, Teachers College, Columbia University.

MARANELL, G. M. (1968), 'A factor analytic study of some selected dimensions of religious attitude ', *Sociology and Social Research*, vol 52, pp. 430-7.

MARETT, R. R. (1914), *The Threshold of Religion*, London, Methuen.

MARWICK, A. (1970), *The Nature of History*, Macmillan.

MATLOCK, D. T. (1973), 'The social psychology of prejudice: The religious syndrome and a belief in free will ', *Dissertation Abstracts*, vol. 33 (7-A), pp. 3375-6.

MEREDITH, G. M. (1959), 'Religious affiliation and self-conception among Japanese-American college women ', *Psychological Reports*, vol 5, p. 543.

MOBERG, D. O. (1970), 'Theological position and institutional characteristics of Protestant congregations ', *Journal for the Scientific Study of Religion*, vol. 9 (1), pp. 53-8.

NADELL, S. F. (1951), *The Foundations of Social Anthropology*, Glencoe, Ill., The Free Press.

NATHAN, M. (1932), *The Attitude of the Jewish Student in the Colleges and Universities towards his Religion*, Block.

NELSON, G. K. (1972), 'The membership of a cult : the spiritualist national union ', *Review of Religious Research*, vol. 13 (3), pp. 170-7.

NELSON, M. O., and JONES, E. M. (1958), 'An application of the Q-technique to the study of religious concepts ', *Psychological Reports*, vol. 3, pp. 293-7.

OLT, R. (1956), *An Approach to the Psychology of Religion*, Christopher.

OSGOOD, C. E. (1953), *Method and Theory in Experimental Psychology*, Oxford University Press.

OSSER, H. A., OSTWALD, P. F., MACWHINNEY, B., and CASEY, R. L. (1973), 'Glossolalia speech from a psycholinguistic perspective ', *Journal of Psycholinguistic Research*, vol. 2 (1), pp. 9-19.

PAHNKE, W. N. (1966), 'Drugs and Mysticism ', *International Journal of Parapsychology*, vol. 8 (2), pp. 295-314.

PANG, H. (1968), 'Religious attitudes of students ', *Psychological Reports*, vol. 22, p. 344.

PARRY, H. J. (1949), 'Protestants, Catholics and prejudice ', *International Journal of Opinion and Research*, vol. 3, pp. 205-13.

PAVLOV, I. P. (1927), *Conditioned Reflexes*, translation by ANREP, G. V., Oxford University Press.

PFISTER, D. (1948), *Christianity and Fear*, Macmillan.

PHOTIADIS, J. D., and BIGGAR, J. (1962), 'Religiosity, education and ethnic distance ', *American Journal of Sociology*, vol. 67, pp. 666-72.

PHOTIADIS, J. D., and JOHNSON, A. L. (1963), 'Orthodoxy, church participation and authoritarianism ', *American Journal of Sociology*, vol. 69, pp. 244-8.

PIAGET, J. (1958), *The Growth of Logical Thinking from Childhood to Adolescence*, Routledge and Kegan Paul.

PILKINGTON, G. W., POPPLETON, P. K., and ROBERTSHAW, G. (1965), 'Changes in religious attitudes and practices among students during university degree courses', *British Journal of Educational Psychology*, vol. 35, pp. 150-57.

POPE, L. (1948), 'Religion and the class structure', *Annals of the American Academy of Political and Social Science*, vol. 256, pp. 84-91.

POPPLETON, P. K., and PILKINGTON, G. W. (1963), 'The measurement of religious attitudes', *British Journal of Social and Clinical Psychology*, vol. 2 (1), pp. 20-36.

PRATT, J. B. (1924), *The Religious Consciousness*, Macmillan.

PRATT, K. C. (1937), 'Differential selection of intelligence according to denominational preference of college freshmen', *Journal of Social Psychology*, vol. 8, pp. 301-10.

PRINCE, A. J. (1971), 'Attitudes of Catholic university students in the U.S. towards Catholic-Protestant intermarriage, *International Journal of Sociology of the Family*, vol. 1 Special Issue, pp. 99-126.

RANCK, J. G. (1955), *Some Personality Correlates of Religious Attitude and Belief*, Ph.D. dissertation, Columbia University.

RASCHKE, V. (1973), 'Dogmatism and religiosity, committed and consensual', *Journal for the Scientific Study of Religion*, vol. 12 (3), pp. 339-44.

RAY-CHOWDHURY, K. (1958), 'Allport-Vernon study of values (old form) in Indian situation: I. Religious group differences in values' *Indian Psychological Bulletin*, vol. 3, pp. 55-67.

Readers Digest (1972) *Great World Atlas*.

RHODES, A. L. (1960), 'Authoritarianism and fundamentalism of rural and urban high school students', *Journal of Educational Sociology*, vol. 34, pp. 97-105.

RHODES, A. L., and NAM, C. B. (1970), 'The religious context of educational expectations', *American Sociological Review*, vol. 35, pp. 253-67.

RICHARDSON, J. T. (1973), 'Psychological interpretation of glossolalia: a reexamination of research', *Journal for the Scientific Study of Religion*, vol, 12 (2), pp. 199-207.

ROGERS, D. P. (1966), 'Some regligious beliefs of scientists and the effect of the scientific method', *Review of Religious Research*, vol. 7 (2), pp. 70-7.

ROKEACH, M. (1960), *The Open and Closed Mind*, Basic Books.

ROSTEN, L. (1955), *A Guide to the Religions of America*, Simon and Schuster.

SAPPENFIELD, B. R. (1942), 'The attitudes of Catholic, Protestant and Jewish students', *Journal of Social Psychology*, vol. 16, pp. 173-97.

SARGANT, W. (1957), *Battle for the Mind*, Heineman.

SCHULL, W. J., YANASE, T., and NEMOTO, H. (1962), 'Kuroshima: the impact of religion on the island's genetic heritage', *Human Biology*, vol. 34 (4), pp. 271-98.

SCOBIE, G. E. W. (1967), *Personality Factors in Religious Belief and Behaviour*, M.Sc. dissertation, Bristol University.

SCOBIE, G. E. W. (1973), 'Types of Christian conversion', *Journal of Behavioural Science*, vol. 1 (5), pp. 265-71.

SHAND, J. D. (1968), 'A twenty-year follow-up study of the religious beliefs of 114 Amherst college students', *Dissertation Abstracts*, vol. 28 (11-A), p. 4753.

SINCLAIR, R. D. (1928), 'A comparative study of those who report the experience of the Divine presence and those who do not', *University of Iowa Studies: Study of Character*, vol. 2, no. 3, p. 63.

SLATER, E. (1947), 'Neurosis and religious affiliation', *Journal of Mental Science*, vol. 93, pp. 392-8.

SMITH, M. B., BRUNER, J. S., and WHITE, R. W., (1956), *Opinions and Personality*, Wiley.

SPAULDING, K. E. (1972), 'The theology of the pew', *Review of Religious Research*, vol. 13 (3), pp. 206-11.

SPINKS, G. S. (1960), *Fundamentals of Religious Belief*, Hodder and Stoughton.

SPINKS, G. S. (1963), *Psychology and Religion: An Introduction to Contemporary Views*, Methuen.

STANLEY, G. (1963), 'Personality and attitude characteristics of fundamentalist theological students', *Australian Journal of Psychology*, vol. 15 (2), pp. 121-3.

STANLEY, G. (1963), 'Personality and attitude characteristics of fundamentalist university students', *Australian Journal of Psychology*, vol. 15 (3), pp. 199-200.

STARBUCK, E. D. (1899), *The Psychology of Religion*, Walter Scott.

STARBUCK, E. D. (1926), 'An empirical study of mysticism', *Proceedings of the 6th International Congress of Philosophy*, pp. 87-94.

Statesman's Year Book 1973-74.

STEININGER, M. P., DURSO, B. E., and PASQUARIELLO, C, (1972), 'Dogmatism and attitudes', *Psychological Reports*, vol. 30 (1), pp. 151-7.

STEWART, R. A., and WEBSTER, A. C. (1970), 'Scale for theological conservatism and its personality correlates', *Perceptual and Motor Skills*, vol. 30, pp. 867-70.

STRICKLAND, B. R., and WEDDELL, S. C. (1972), 'Religious orientation, racial prejudice and dogmatism: a study of Baptists and Unitarians', *Journal for the Scientific Study of Religion*, vol. 11 (4), pp. 395-9.

SUTKER, P. B., SUTKER, L. W., and KILPATRICK, D. G. (1970), 'Religious preference, practice and personal sexual attitudes and behaviour', *Psychological Reports*, vol. 26, pp. 835-41.

SYMINGTON, T. A. (1935), 'Religious liberals and conservatives', *Teachers' College Contributions to Education*, no. 640.

TAPP, R. B. (1971), 'Dimensions of religiosity in a post-traditional group', *Journal for the Scientific Study of Religion*, vol. 10 (1), pp. 41-7.

THOULESS, R. H. (1923), *An Introduction to the Psychology of Religion*, Cambridge University Press (1971) Third Edition.

THOULESS, R. H. (1935), 'The tendency to certainty in religious belief', *British Journal of Psychology*, vol. 26, pp. 16-31.

THOULESS, R. H. (1954), *Authority and Freedom*, Hodder and Stoughton.

THURSTON, L. L. (1931), *Scale for the Measurement of Attitude towards Evolution*, University of Chicago Press.

TRANKELL, A. (1972), *The Reliability of Evidence*, Bechmans, Stockholm.

TRENAMAN, J. (1952), *Out of Step*, Methuen.

WALLACE, R. K., (1970), ' Physiological effects of transcendental meditation ', *Science*, no. 167, pp. 1751-4.

WALLIN, P. (1957), ' Religiosity, sexual gratification, and marital satisfaction ', *American Sociological Review*, vol. 22, pp. 300-5.

WALLIN, P., and CLARK, A. L. (1964), ' Religiosity, sexual gratification and marital satisfaction in the middle years of marriage ', *Social Forces*, vol. 42 (3), pp. 303-9.

WEARING, A. J., and BROWN, L. B. (1972), 'The dimensionality of religion ', *British Journal of Social and Clinical Psychology*, vol 11 (2), pp. 143-8.

WEBB, S. C. (1965), ' An exploratory investigation of some needs met through religious behaviour ', *Journal for the Scientific Study of Religion*, vol. 5, pp. 51-8.

WEBER, M. (1904-5), *The Protestant Ethic and the Spirit of Capitalism*, translation by Parsons, T., Allen and Unwin, 1930.

WEBER, M. (1922), in *Sociology of Religion*, by Mohr, J. C. B., Paul Siebeck.

WELFORD, A. T. (1947), ' Is religious behaviour dependent upon effect or frustration?', *Journal of Abnormal and Social Psychology*, vol. 42, pp. 310-19.

WELFORD, A. T. (1971), *Christianity: A Psychologist's Translation*, Hodder and Stoughton.

WILKERSON, D. (1963), *The Cross and the Switchblade*, New Jersey, Spire Books.

WILSON, B. R. (1961), *Sects and Society*, Heinemann.

WILSON, G. R. (1973), *The Psychology of Conservatism*, Academic Press.

WILSON, W. C. (1960), ' Extrinsic religious values and prejudice ', *Journal of Abnormal and Social Psychology*, vol. 60, pp. 286-8.

WILSON, W. P. (1972), 'Mental health benefits of religious salvation ', *Diseases of the Nervous System*, vol. 33 (6), pp. 382-6.

WOODWARD, E. W. (1932), ' Relations of religious training and life patterns to the adult religious life ', *Teachers' College Contributions to Education*, no. 527.

YINGER, J. M. (1957), *Religion, Society and the Individaul*, Macmillan.

YINGER, J. M. (1970), *The Scientific Study of Religion*, Macmillan.

ZUKERMAN, M., KOLIN, E. A., PRICE, L., and ZOOB, I. (1964), ' Development of a sensation-seeking scale ', *Journal of Consulting Psychology*, vol. 28, pp. 477-80.

Index

Index 183

dependence, 28

Devil, 99

development, 149, 160, 164, 169

development, moral, 147
stage, 147

Dice, L. R., et al, 45

Di Guiseppe, R. A., 117

dimensional, uni-, 60, 61f, 154
multi-, 60, 61f, 63, 103, 154, 160, 167

dimensions, 58, 61, 62ff, 69, 76, 78, 79, 92, 93, 94, 95, 134, 159
unipolar, 62, 63
bipolar, 62, 63, 72

discipleship, 67

Dittes, J. E., 39, 61, 62

doctrine, 23, 68, 117, 134, 165

dogma, 68

dogmatism, 48, 70, 76, 78, 115, 116, 117, 122, 155, 160, 161

dreams, 88

Dreger, R. M., 73, 113

drugs, 37, 88, 89, 101, 152, 167

Durkheim, E., 103, 126

Eastern Orthodox Church, 82, 83

economics, 108

ecstatic utterances, 90

Eddy, J. P., 140

education, 118, 130, 132, 138ff, 142, 143, 144, 145, 148, 149, 150

emotion, 26, 50, 137f, 150, 151, 158, 162

emotionalism, 91ff

emotionality, 91

Episcopal Church, 42, 44, 83, 90, 118, 166

epistemology, 20, 21

Estus, C. W., et al, 128, 129

eternal life, 11

ethic, 111, 130, 132

ethical code, 10, 144

ethical injunction, 12

ethics, 21, 79, 84, 126, 161

ethnocentrism, 113, 115, 116, 117

evaluation 154ff

evangelical, 71

evangelism, 9, 10, 47, 52, 68ff, 107, 119, 145, 148, 151, 152, 164

evangelist, 151ff

evangelistic meetings 36, 73

existential, 25

existential philosophy, 26
psychology, 26, 32, 168

existentialism, 26

experiments
field, 34
laboratory, 33
natural, 34, 35

extraversion, 6, 122, 158, 159, 160

Eysenck, H. J., 49, 58, 63, 77, 112, 119, 120, 121, 122, 123, 124, 158

factors, 63

factor analysis, 37, 58ff, 100, 109, 167

faith, 8, 10, 66, 149, 150, 151

faith healing, 90

family, 131

fantasy, 54

father, 98

father figure, 97, 98

Faulkner, J. E., et al, 69

fear, 80, 107, 151, 152, 159, 160, 162

fellowship, 81
meal, 9, 81

feminine role, 110, 111, 156, 157

Ferguson, L. W., 58

Ferm, R. O., 106

Festinger, L., 100

Fetter, G. C., 41

field studies, 34, 35

Fischer, H., et al, 60

Fisher, S. C., 131

flagellation, 88

Flew, A., et al, 22

Flower, J. C., 99

Flugel, J. C., 98, 99

forgiveness, 9, 84, 86, 99

France, 133

Frazer, J., 17

Freud, S., 28, 83, 97, 98

frustration, 104, 105, 159

frustration theory, 97, 98

Fry, C. L., 42, 118, 119

functional theory, 126

fundamentalism, 46, 56, 61, 70, 72, 73, 94, 117, 134, 143, 145, 158

genuinely devout, 30, 121, 136, 137, 165, 167